D1578097

DISCOURSES ON DANTE

Discourses on Dante

BY

CHARLES H. GRANDGENT

NEW YORK / RUSSELL & RUSSELL

FIRST PUBLISHED IN 1924 BY HARVARD UNIVERSITY PRESS

REISSUED, 1970, BY RUSSELL & RUSSELL

A DIVISION OF ATHENEUM PUBLISHERS, INC.

BY ARRANGEMENT WITH HARVARD UNIVERSITY PRESS

L. C. CATALOG CARD NO: 75-102496

PRINTED IN THE UNITED STATES OF AMERICA

Preface

HERE are gathered various addresses and poems that cluster about the sexcentenary year, 1921. This volume may be regarded, then, as a small and rather belated tribute to the world-wide commemoration of the great poet. Most of the things here offered have appeared before, in journal, report, or program. The sestina was printed in the *Atlantic Monthly* for September, 1921; the sonnet, in a pamphlet, *The Exercises in the Auditorium of the National Museum at Washington, Commemorative of the Sexcentenary of the Death of Dante Alighieri*, which contained also "Dante Six Hundred Years After." "Dante and Italy" saw the light in *Columbus* for December, 1920, and February and April, 1921; "Illumination" and "Dante's Verse," in *Studies in Philology*, October, 1921, and January, 1920; "The Centre of the Circle," in the *Harvard Alumni Bulletin* for January 5, 1922. The greater part of "All Men Naturally Desire to Know" was published as an article, "Dante, Scholar and Philosopher," in the *Revue Néo-Scholastique* of Louvain, in February,

1922. "The Choice of a Theme" came out in the *Thirty-Seventh Annual Report of the Dante Society* of Cambridge, Mass., in 1920. To the editors of these publications I gratefully acknowledge my indebtedness for permission to reprint. "Lost Poems of Dante" is quite new.

C. H. G.

Contents

Chapter I

THE FOURTEENTH OF SEPTEMBER
1321–1921

AS age, their shadow, follows life and birth,
So autumn shadowed summertime and spring
And day was yielding fast to equal night,
When, homeward soaring from the rustling shore
Where weary Po exchanges life for peace,
His spring-born spirit fled, so long ago.

Six slowly winding centuries ago,
Reborn was he in everlasting birth,
To taste the food for which he hungered, peace,
At marriage suppers set in endless spring,
Shoresman eternal on the radiant shore
Which never saw its sun engulft in night.

A sinful world of self-created night
He left behind, so many years ago,
A world where hatred ruled from shore to shore
And men, despite their gentle Saviour's birth,
Like ancient Adam forfeited their spring,
For greed and discord bartering their peace.

To light the day of universal peace,
God-sent he dawned upon our bloody night,
Greatest of poets since the primal spring
Flasht forth into existence long ago.
Benignant stars presided o'er his birth,
That he might speak to every listening shore.

Still rings his voice on ocean's either shore,
And when he speaks, our Muses hold their peace
And wonder if the world shall see the birth
Of man like him before the Judgment night,
For all he died so many years ago,
When this our iron age was in its spring.

Ere winter blossom into balmy spring,
Ere peace prevail on any mortal shore
(So taught the Tuscan poet long ago),
Justice must reign: in it alone is peace.
The Hound shall chase the Wolf into the night,
Then earth and heaven shall witness a rebirth.

Heaven gave him birth, one ever-blessed spring,
Whose lamp through all the night illumes our shore.
He found his peace six hundred years ago.

Chapter II

DANTE SIX HUNDRED YEARS AFTER

SIX HUNDRED years is a long while, more than four times the whole life of our Nation. Call back to mind, one after another, the vicissitudes of our Republic, the succession of parties and of burning questions, the generations of statesmen, the steady march of population from the Atlantic to the Pacific, the great disruption and subsequent reunion, the change from isolation on a distant shore to close neighborhood in all the world's affairs, the transformation of industry and society by steam, by electricity, by chemistry; and multiply the sum of all this by four. It is a long time for a poet's work to live.

Six hundred years ago the whole known world was clustered together on one quarter of the earth's surface; the rest was all emptiness, fearful, yet alluring in its mystery; and by far the greater portion, even of the lands whereof men spoke, was a realm of myth, peopled by weird creatures, the offspring of imagination. In those days our globe, forever still, stood at the centre of the universe, which formed a bigger sphere around it; circling about the earth were sundry transparent heavens, one beyond the other, carrying in their rotations the celestial bodies perceptible to the human eye. Such was Dante's world, a world which, according to the best science of that age, had lasted but a few thousand years and was to last but a few hundred years longer, its entire history, its entire existence being packed into a period of some seven thousand years, between Creation and Judgment Day. Had Dante been told that his fame would endure six hundred years, he would have smiled incredulously; for he did not believe the world would last so long.

Small as was Dante's physical world in space and in time, correspondingly great was the sense of infinity beyond. The less room given to matter, the more room open to spirit; the more petty the bulk of mundane affairs, the vaster the scope of wonder and of worship. The abstract, the spiritual, the divine loomed gigantic in proportion to the puny earth. On the other hand, the little finite round universe known to man was better and more generally known than is our immense, shapeless, unimaginable universe of to-day. Not the astronomer alone, but the laborer, even the man of letters, knew all the stars, and when they rose and when they set and how their orbits were related. When lamps were scarce, the lights of heaven were more precious; when clocks and calendars were few, close heed was given to the great dial of the sky.

Such was the world, and such was man, six hundred years ago. In all the material aspects of civilization, humanity was far closer to ancient Egypt, or to ancient Babylon, than to the conditions in which we live. For science, advancing at a rate of multiplying acceleration, has in the last two centuries alone made more progress than in all the hundreds of thousands of years during which a human race has existed on our planet. Science, physical science, it is that has so wonderfully expanded, and in its expansion transformed the external features of life. But science is not wisdom; and in wisdom who shall say that we have advanced at all? Is not the world just as foolish as ever, and just as wicked? Do men think more rationally or act more unselfishly? It were prudent not to press the question, lest the answer prove to be worse than a simple negative. Who shall say that men, in two hundred, in six hundred, nay, in two thousand years, have in the least improved their knowledge and their understanding of one another? Who shall affirm that they have gained in artistry? Who shall deny that since Dante's day they have immeasurably lost in spiritual intuition?

Such as it was, better on one side, worse on another, similar to our experience in some things, bafflingly unlike in other, more obvious ones, Dante's age lies six hundred years behind us, in a remote, all but forgotten past. Yet out of that hazy distance calls a voice — not a voice that is faint and fading, but a tone that like an organ note swells louder and ever louder as the centuries go on. It is the voice of a poet, calling from his age to ours. What means its persistent appeal? Why should we be stirred to the very depths by the voice of a world that had so little in common with ours? For the caller is not even one of the vanished mighty: no king, no prelate; only a poet. Only a citizen of a little city, long ago, when nations were just beginning to take shape; not even a citizen all his days, but for his last twenty years an outcast, dependent on chance and charity. Why must we listen to his call?

Other great voices still reach us from the past, from a past equally far away, or farther; but they are sustained and reinforced by circumstance. We lend ear to the prophets of the Old Testament, to the voice that rises from Patmos, because we believe them to be spokesmen of God; they are a part of the Christian religion, and as long as that religion shall last, they cannot fail to find a hearing. We still hearken (though less and less willingly) to Homer, to Sophocles, to Virgil, because they belong to the tradition of the schools; they are, or have been, a part of occidental education; they persist as long as the classical ideal maintains itself; but as the old humanities unhappily lose their hold, those grand, sweet voices grow faint and distant, to the irreparable loss of educated men. Dante's immortality is assured by no similar support: he is neither an acknowledged prophet of the Church nor an accepted textbook of the schools; he is only a poet, singing all alone. But when he calls, we listen.

We listen, first of all, because the sweetness of that voice compels us. Like the voice of the Siren in the poet's dream, it "wholly satisfies" us, and, when once we have caught it, we cannot turn away. Gently rippling, voluptuous, limpid, grand, majestic, terrible by turns, it varies endlessly, as does the flow of human emotion; it answers every longing of the human heart. And, with all its beauty, it is never empty sound: not a phrase, not a word is without its message, a message worthy of remembrance and reflection. Never was poem more compactly written than the *Divine Comedy;* never was a work of art more heavily freighted with thought. And never, in the whole realm of art, was another work conceived with such daring, such sublime imagination. Other poets have dulcetly recorded past impressions; others, more original, have concocted novel compounds of old sensations and ideas; but to Dante it was reserved to conceive a new world of the intangible, to lend actual presence to the immaterial, to create a Heaven with no earthly ingredients save light and music, a kingdom of love and gladness eternal, infinite in extent, endless in variety, perfect in the fitness of its many mansions. Never before, and never since, has art brought mankind so close to pure spirit.

Sheer beauty, then, beauty captivating, enthralling, uplifting, is the first secret of Dante's charm. But there are more secrets in his magic. To our curiosity the enchanter unfolds the whole panorama of a departed time, the whole world of the Middle Ages, so picturesque in its distance, so different from ours in its external aspect, yet at heart, in many regards, so like. Looking back over the great epochs of human history, we seek in vain for another period represented with comparable fulness and vitality in a single masterpiece of art. The Homeric Age would doubtless come next, in the order of poetic interpretation; but the *Iliad*, with all its beauty, shows forth only a few sides of human life in the Homeric world. Whereas the *Divine Comedy*, understandingly read, evokes a picture of medieval existence in its completeness, with its great aspirations, religious, social, philosophical, artistic, with the intricacies of its politics, the rivalry of municipal interests, the hates and loves of all sorts and conditions of men.

But that is not all. Not only does Dante's poem reveal to us a dead age: it reveals a living man, a man who, as long as our civilization shall last, can never die. Discreetly reticent in all that pertains to his bodily career, Dante opens wide the windows of his soul. Always, behind the majestic verses, we see the man, eager, intense, sensitive, vibrating to every touch, forceful, independent in thought and fearless

in act, intelligent and imaginative far beyond his
fellows, goaded by insatiable curiosity, learned but
ever craving to learn more, reverent toward divine,
but critical of worldly authority, adoring God with
all his heart and abhorring God's enemies, a whole-
souled lover of the good and an unmitigated hater
of the bad. And this man had eyes not only to observe and judge society, to catch the salient traits of
individuals and human types, but also to appreciate
the wonders of nature, on earth and in the sky.

And he had voice to sing of what he saw. With a
few deft strokes he can set vividly before us the
whole personality of a man, or all the loveliness or all
the wildness of a landscape. Who can forget the
haughty figure of the lost heretic, Farinata degli
Uberti, who stood amid the flames "with breast and
brow erect, as held he Hell in great contempt," —

> Ed ei s' ergea col petto e colla fronte,
> Come avesse lo inferno in gran dispitto;
> > [*Inf.*, x, 35–36.]

the majestic Sordello, who, " like a lion at rest," sat
" all alone, proud and scornful, dignified and slow in
the turning of his eyes," —

> Venimmo a lei.   O anima Lombarda,
>   Come ti stavi altera e disdegnosa
>   E nel mover degli occhi onesta e tarda!
> Ella non ci diceva alcuna cosa;
>   Ma lasciavane gir, solo sguardando
>   A guisa di leon, quando si posa;
> > [*Purg.*, vi, 61–66.]

or those faint spirits of nuns, so evanescent that they seem reflections of our faces " in clean, transparent window-panes, or in waters pure and still, but not so deep that the depths are dark"? —

> Quali per vetri trasparenti e tersi
>   O ver per acque nitide e tranquille,
>   Non sì profonde che i fondi sien persi,
> Tornan dei nostri visi le postille
>   Debili sì che perla in bianca fronte
>   Non vien men tosto alle nostre pupille,
> Tali vid' io più facce a parlar pronte.
>
> [*Par.*, III, 10–16.]

They are as unforgettable as the distant rumble of the waterfall, "like the hum that beehives make," —

> Già era in loco ove s' udia il rimbombo
>   Dell' acqua che cadea nell' altro giro,
>   Simile a quel che l' arnie fanno rombo;
>
> [*Inf.*, XVI, 1–3.]

the sun's disk gradually showing itself through mountain mists; the slowly falling flakes of snow in the Alps; the morning breeze on the ocean, chased by the dawn, until the eye beholds "afar the rippling of the sea," —

> L' alba vinceva l' ôra mattutina
>   Che fuggia innanzi, sì che di lontano
>   Conobbi il tremolar della marina;
>
>   [*Purg.*, I, 115–117.]

the forest foliage, in the morning wind, all bending to the west, but not so stirred as to deter "the little

birds in the tree-tops from plying all their art, the
birdlets that with full-throated gladness greeted the
early hours amid the leaves, which bore such burden
to their songs as one catches in the pine-grove on the
shore of Classe," when the southeast wind is set free.

> Un' aura dolce, senza mutamento
>   Avere in sè, mi feria per la fronte
>   Non di più colpo che soave vento;
> Per cui le fronde, tremolando pronte,
>   Tutte quante piegavano alla parte
>   U' la prim' ombra gitta il santo monte;
> Non però dal lor esser dritto sparte
>   Tanto che gli augelletti per le cime
>   Lasciasser d' operare ogni lor arte,
> Ma con piena letizia l'ore prime,
>   Cantando, ricevièno intra le foglie,
>   Che tenevan bordone alle sue rime
> Tal qual di ramo in ramo si raccoglie
>   Per la pineta in sul lito di Chiassi
>   Quand' Eolo Scirocco fuor discioglie.
>   [*Purg.*, xxviii, 7–21.]

Not alone in swift, unerring description does
Dante excel, but in all the devices of literary art: in
climax, in contrast, in suspense, in surprise. In dra-
matic power many of the episodes of his *Hell* and
Purgatory have never been surpassed. What the
poet saw—and he saw as few men have seen—he
makes us see.

And again and ever, beyond all the figures of his
imagining, he makes us see himself, solitary, keen,
and thoughtful, filled to overflowing with love for
his Maker and his Maker's glorious universe, full of

indignation at the perversity of man; an unflinching champion of justice, which, he declares, is naught else than God's will; a prophet who became the national genius of a great people, and by his irresistible attraction collecting its dissevered members, led it at last out of Egypt into the Promised Land of union and freedom. This is the Dante that Italians love; and their love and their admiration the whole world shares to-day.

Many things draw us to him. Among them is his devoted pursuit of knowledge, of truth. Recognizing, with his masters, Aristotle and St. Thomas, that man differs from the brutes by the gift of intelligence, which forever impels him to learn, even as instinct moves the lower creatures to fulfil their several humbler missions (inasmuch as the craving for knowledge is, so to speak, the instinct of an intelligent being), Dante declares that man can never find contentment save in the endeavor to fill the endless hunger of his mind, to approach the constantly receding goal of omniscience. All knowledge Dante took for his field, and, in so far as it was attainable, he made it all his own.

Knowledge was for him no aggregation of unrelated facts; the individual items were but parts of an immense and logically adjusted system, the system of God's universe. The business of science is, in the words of a recent author, "to make plainer the way from one thing to the whole of things." While the whole of things must forever elude our limited vision, we can, if we will, apprehend enough of its wholeness to discern, though dimly, the infinite wisdom and love and power that planned it all. In all the world — the world of matter, the world of spirit, the world of man, who is both matter and spirit — Dante sought and found a revelation of God. Philosophy is but the handmaid of religion, the intellectual approach to intuition. In the face of Lady Philosophy, he affirms, "I mean in her eyes and in her sweet smile, appear things which reveal the joys of Paradise, things which Love carries thither as to their own place. They overpower our understanding, as a sunbeam overpowers a feeble eye; and inasmuch as I cannot gaze upon them fixedly, I must be content to say little of them. . . . She was conceived by Him who set the universe in motion." (*Convivio*, Canzone II, 55–72.)

Not to be able to "gaze fixedly," not to have vision to grasp the whole of things, was one of Dante's sorest trials, a privation which to bear with patience required all the piety of his loving submission to the heavenly will. With quick, incessant inquisitiveness he was forever peering into the great mystery; and every bit of truth he won seemed to bring him a step nearer the inaccessible goal. Not only in its vast outlines, but in its smallest details as well, he looked upon the universe as a manifestation of the divine mind. Meditating on the skies, which

he loved to study, — for his favorite science was
astronomy, — he found in the exact angle at which
the ecliptic crosses the equator a proof of infinite
foresight; for the precise degree of its acuteness
carries the sun's annual pathway over that part of
the earth where it is most beneficial to man. Ob-
serving the habits of birds, of which he was so fond,
he saw in their nest-building — an activity pursued
with perfect confidence though without model or
master — a tiny image of the creative act of God.
On every hand, the more he looked, the more he detected in the universe images or symbols of things
spiritual and divine. And in symbols, appropriately
conceived and beautifully wrought, he, following the
mode of his Church and his age, chose to convey to
the reader his philosophical thoughts, his spiritual
struggles. Hence the vesture of allegory, which in
Dante's *New Life* veils as a gauze the happenings
recorded in that youthful autobiography, but which
fully clothes in symbolic garments the psychic story
of the *Divine Comedy*.

Allegory, sustained allegory, as a literary method,
has passed from fashion, and the modern reader experiences some difficulty in adjusting his mind to so
unfamiliar a means of presentation. With Dante's
intellectual curiosity, on the other hand, he is in full
sympathy; he can therefore understand the tormenting "desire to know," the endless chase after
the causes of things, the reaching out for truths so

subtle that they can be grasped only in the form of symbols and can find expression only in allegorical terms. One of the chief joys of Heaven — so Dante believes — is the quenching of that "concreated and perpetual thirst," the draught of the eternal water of truth, the only water that satisfies. His vision of Paradise culminates in one instant of perfect comprehension, as his will and his desire merge in the everlasting "Love that moves the sun and the other stars."

After all, it is no wonder that Dante's name has been held in reverence for six hundred years. He did things too great, and was himself too great, to lapse into oblivion, even with the changes of six centuries. There is too much of the universal in his message, too much that belongs to all time. [He is the poet of all the generations of men, and no age may appropriate him to itself alone.] Has he, then, no spiritual message for us, nothing on which we may base a particular claim? We should dearly like to attach him to ourselves: our generation has held him in higher esteem than any generation before; and we are sorely in need of a prophet.

Our need is dire indeed. For we men and women of the present moment are sunk in one of those moral depressions that always follow violent crises of moral exhilaration. Poor humanity, it would seem, has not the endurance to maintain itself at a high level, when the stress is over. After the years

of fiery patriotism, of self-sacrifice, of consecration
to ideals, comes a period of reaction, an era of ma-
terialistic selfishness, of cynicism, of callous distrust
and indifference. Such was the aftermath of our
Civil War, as some of us can still remember. Such
is the disheartening epilogue of the great tragedy in
which we have just played a part. Tired of heroics,
disappointed in our expectations, we drop from
zenith to nadir, ashamed to listen to our better
selves. We need a mighty voice or a grand example
to restore our courage. Can we find, in the poet
whom we honor to-day, no voice, no example that
seems addressed to us, nothing to guide us back to
the heights we have forsaken, no motto to inscribe
on our banners?

The motto is there, in Dante's poem and in his
life. Far older than Dante, it consists of three words:
faith, hope, charity. Ere the dreamer of the *Divine
Comedy* can enter the true Paradise, the blessed goal
of all his striving, the sequel to his Hell and Purgatory, he must confirm himself in these three Christian virtues. At the behest of St. Peter, St. James,
and St. John, he avows and defines them. Of his
charity — of all the promptings of his love, strong
or gentle — the alpha and omega, he declares, is
God; the plants in all the garden of the Eternal
Gardener the poet loves in proportion to the degree
of grace bestowed by the Gardener on each. Hope,
whereof "no son of the Church Militant hath more,"

is the certain expectation of blessedness. Faith,
"the substance of things hoped for, the evidence of
things not seen," Dante is conscious of possessing,
plain and firm beyond suspicion of doubt.

Love, says the poet, is rightly directed first and
last to God, from whom all goodness flows. Upon
God's creatures love is rightly turned in proportion
to the likeness they bear to their Maker. Among all
the human beings that Dante ever beheld, the one
in whom God was most clearly revealed was a certain gentle maiden called Beatrice, who appeared to
his wistful eyes a veritable angel on earth, the embodiment of celestial mind; so divine, so Madona-
like was her sweetness, her modest dignity. To her,
next to her Maker, he paid reverent homage; to her
service, as to the service of the Almighty, he dedicated himself after her death. If God should in his
mercy spare the poet's life for a few years, that his
preparation might be sufficient, things such as were
never written of any lady should be sung of the
queen of his soul. Thus runs his promise, at the
close of the *New Life*. The whole *Divine Comedy* is
its fulfilment — a monument such as no other man
ever erected to any woman. Beatrice, however, is
glorified, not for her perishable charms, but for the
indwelling godliness that radiates from her, leading men heavenward with its kindly light. She is
cherished and exalted, not as a mortal woman, but
as a guide to the universal Father. The real object

of Dante's loving glorification is God himself; to
"the glory of Him who moveth all," —

La gloria di Colui che tutto move, —

the *Divine Comedy* is really dedicated, a tribute
to divine justice, divine love, divine wisdom. If
Dante's *Hell* may be described as the Tragedy of Sin,
if his *Purgatory* has been called the Epic of Free Will,
we may name his *Paradise*, that triumphant procla-
mation of God's mysterious but perfect plan, the
Hymn of Predestination.

Hope follows love and faith, without which it
could not sustain itself. Seldom has man's hope
been more sorely tried than was Dante's. For
brave, honest, fair-minded patriotism his reward
was exile, poverty, separation from his family, peril
of death by fire, calumny. "Ever since it was the
pleasure of the citizens of Florence, that most beautiful and most famous daughter of Rome, to cast me
out of her sweetest bosom, wherein I was born and
bred, and where, with their good leave, I long with
all my heart to rest my weary mind and end my
alloted time — ever since then I have wandered as
a stranger, almost as a beggar, over nearly all regions where our language extends, displaying against
my will the wound of fortune, for which ofttimes the
wounded one is wont unjustly to be blamed. Truly
have I been a boat without sail or helm, carried to
divers harbors and inlets and shores by the dry wind
that breathes from painful poverty."

Thus for once, in a single passage of his *Banquet*, the uncomplaining Dante utters a complaint. For he was compelled to learn "how salt is the taste of other men's bread and how hard a path it is to climb up and down other men's stairs." But in the midst of all his misery the exile fondly harbored hope — and not alone the heavenly hope which did not forsake him: a worldly hope as well, though a worthy one, the hope that recognition of his genius, when once his poem should be completed, would move his fellow townsmen to restore him to citizenship and crown him with bay in his old Baptistery of St. John's.

> If fate ordain my sacred poem here,
>   Which heaven and earth so amply have supplied
>   That it hath kept me lean this many a year,
> Shall melt the hate that locketh me outside
>   My pretty fold, where once I slept a lamb
>   Whom hostile wolves with their devices tried,
> With louder voice and fleece of stalwart ram
>   Returning, on mine own baptismal font
>   Shall I be crowned a poet, as I am.

> Se mai continga che il poema sacro,
>   Al quale ha posto mano e cielo e terra
>   Sì che m' ha fatto per più anni macro,
> Vinca la crudeltà che fuor mi serra
>   Del bello ovil dov' io dormii agnello,
>   Nimico ai lupi che gli danno guerra,
> Con altra voce omai, con altro vello
>   Ritornerò poeta, ed in sul fonte
>   Del mio battesmo prenderò il cappello.
>   [*Par.*, xxv, 1–9.]

Faith, among the three virtues, is the one whose lack in our midst is most conspicuous and most disastrous; and it is the one in which Dante most abounds. We need not dwell upon the faith that maintained unshaken his religious doctrine, despite his spirit of scientific inquiry and despite his indignation at the worldliness of prelates: for the teachings of science did but corroborate his creed; and the more unworthy the ministers, the more miraculous is the strength of the Church. Rather let us consider his faith in eternal justice, in the coming of the Kingdom on earth as in Heaven. That advent seemed to him at one time imminent. Amid all the bloody strife and wickedness that surrounded him — due, in his judgment, to a failure of the balance of powers — a new hope dawned upon him, and upon the world, with the election of the Emperor Henry VII, an idealist who assumed the mission of restoring right and reducing the Empire to peace under one government. Dante's Latin letters written in those exciting years give voice to almost frenzied elation and wild, impatient expectation.

"A new day is shining," he writes, "announcing dawn, which already lightens the shades of long calamity. . . . We shall behold the joy awaited, we who long have been night-dwellers in the desert." — "Break, then, thy delay, O new offspring of Isaiah, take to thyself trust from the eyes of the Lord God of Hosts, before whom thou dost act; and lay low this Goliath with the sling of thy wisdom and the stone of thy strength. For with his fall, night and darkness shall cover the camp of the Philistines; the Philistines shall be put to flight, and Israel shall be free. Then our inheritance, whose loss we ceaselessly mourn, shall be restored to us entire." With the triumph of Henry the unjust party shall be dispossessed of Florence, and Dante and his fellow "exiles in Babylon," citizens once more, "shall breathe in peace." "All those who hunger and thirst shall be filled with the light of his rays, and those who love iniquity shall be confounded by his countenance all aflame." (*Epistolae: Universis et singulis Italiae regibus* and *Sanctissimo . . . domino Henrico.*)

Alas! this surging hope was doomed to disappointment, this expectation was not to be fulfilled. After meeting with stubborn opposition, most obstinate on the part of Dante's own city, Henry perished in the midst of his great enterprise, and nothing was accomplished. How heavy was the blow we can guess from the intensity of Dante's nature, from his feverish eagerness, from his certainty of success. Never was faith more severely beset. The great plan for world-unity and world-wide peace seemed shattered beyond repair. The wonderful opportunity had come, and was lost, apparently forever.

What was the plan Dante so dearly cherished? It was the conception of a general super-state, which he called *Imperium*, governing the kingdoms of the earth in justice and in peace. "As we see on a ship," he says, "that various duties and various purposes on board are directed to a single end, namely, to reach the desired harbor by a safe course; and, as each officer directs his own effort to his own object, so there is one who considers all these objects and directs them to the ultimate object of all; and this is the captain, whose voice all must obey. The same thing we see in organizations and armies, in all matters that are directed, as has been said, to one end. Wherefore it is plainly evident that to perfect the universal organization of the human race, there must be one captain, as it were, who, considering the various conditions of the world, and establishing the diverse offices necessary, shall have the office of universal and unquestionable command." A gigantic super-state, no other than the Holy Roman Empire, ordained by God, was to hold the nations in check, settle their disputes, repress their encroachments, and keep perpetual peace. The idea seemed to Dante so self-evident, so manifestly a part of the divine intention, so necessary for the maintenance of justice and tranquillity, that he had no patience with anyone who could oppose it.

Yet the adventure failed, the empire upon which Dante had staked all his earthly hopes. How many men could have borne the disillusionment? How many could have refrained from skepticism, could have held to their faith in everlasting righteousness?

Dante met the test. The divine intent was other than he had imagined; but the divine purpose must exist, and that purpose must be fulfilled. "If it is lawful for me so to speak," the poet cries, "O supreme Jove, that wast crucified for us on earth, are thy just eyes turned elsewhere? Or is it a preparation which thou makest, in the abyss of thy counsel, for some good end quite severed from our understanding?"

> E, se licito m' è, o sommo Giove
>   Che fosti in terra per noi crocifisso,
>   Son li giusti occhi tuoi rivolti altrove?
> O è preparazion, che nell' abisso
>   Del tuo consiglio fai per alcun bene
>   In tutto dall' accorger nostro scisso?
>
> [*Purg.*, vi, 118–123.]

Presumptuous it is for man to seek to fathom the mind of the Almighty, or to flatter himself that the means he has chosen must be the means predestined. "O predestination, how far away is thy root from those eyes which behold not the primal cause entire!"

> O predestinazion, quanto remota
>   È la radice tua da quegli aspetti
>   Che la prima cagion non veggion *tota!*
>
> [*Par.*, xx, 130–132.]

Though it come not in our way, peace on earth is sure to come to men of good will; let us be patient, and repine not though it come in a way "quite severed from our understanding." "Now who art thou," exclaims Dante, "that presumest to sit on the bench to judge things a thousand miles away, with a sight no longer than a span?"

> Or tu chi sei, che vuoi sedere a scranna
> Per giudicar da lungi mille miglia
> Con la veduta corta d' una spanna?
> [*Par.*, xix, 79–81.]

To an overhasty craving for explanation of the mystery of Providence, the great ascetic, Peter Damian, thus replies, in Dante's heaven of Saturn: "Whatsoever soul is most illumined in the sky, whatsoever Seraph looks most intently into God, could not respond to thy question; for what thou askest sinks so far beyond in the abyss of the eternal statute that it is removed from every created eye."

> Ma quell' alma nel ciel che più si schiara,
>   Quel Serafin che in Dio più l' occhio ha fisso,
>   Alla domanda tua non satisfara;
> Perocchè sì s' inoltra nell' abisso
>   Dell' eterno statuto quel che chiedi
>   Che da ogni creata vista è scisso.
> [*Par.*, xxi, 91–96.]

Thus Dante reacts to the bitterest disappointment; such is the lesson in faith that he teaches us to-day, six hundred years after his death. Though the world be not saved from wickedness and war in exactly the manner that we may have expected, it will be saved; for justice and righteousness must prevail. Some time, he prophesies, "the ships shall turn stem to stern and the fleet shall sail a true course, and real fruit shall come after the flower."

> Che la fortuna che tanto s' aspetta
>   Le poppe volgerà u' son le prore,
>   Sì che la classe correrà diretta;
> E vero frutto verrà dopo il fiore.
>   [*Par.*, xxvii, 145–148.]

With faith undiminished — nay, increased — but with self-assurance humbled, with a profounder sense of ignorance and of submission to a higher intelligence, Dante confidently waits for a door to open in some quarter unforeseen, content to concur in the Creator's plan, whatever it may be; for "in His will is our peace."

> In la sua volontade è nostra pace.

Chapter III

DANTE AND ITALY

I

THIS year New England celebrates the three-hundredth anniversary of the landing of the Pilgrims in Plymouth, the dawn of a new era for the New World. Next year the nations of the earth will celebrate the six-hundredth anniversary of the death of Dante, an event which marks the close of a very old epoch in the Old World. If we date our own age, as we should, back to the days of the discovery and first settlement of America, and if, as will probably seem right to the men of the future, we regard it as ending with the World War, we shall find it extending over some four hundred years. Gloriously ushered in by an Italian, Columbus, it was brought to a disastrous finish by William, the Prussian. On the other hand, the epoch generally known as the Middle Ages, whose beginnings had been shaped by the powerful hand of Charlemagne, the Frank, after a stretch of more than five hundred years majestically closed with the song of another Italian, Dante Alighieri.

In the modern period, opened by Columbus, has occurred most of the scientific and industrial progress of mankind. To it belong all the developments

of steam and electricity which have so utterly transformed our existence. Of the great inventions that
have raised our material condition above that of
savages, only two antedate our epoch: the wheel,
which facilitates transportation by land; the bow-
line which, enabling mariners to sail against the
wind, makes a highway of the ocean. We may add
to these, as notable but lesser acquisitions of ante-
cedent ages (but subsequent to the savage state),
the compass, the clock, the organ, the alphabet, the
Arabic numerals. Printing and gunpowder, also,
came before our time, but not long before. All the
rest is new — the conception of the universe, all
chemistry, nearly all physics, biology, and medicine,
all the application of great natural forces to the
uses of man.

What claim to recognition has the era that ended
with Dante? Although it did contribute the bow-
line, the compass, the clock, the organ, and the
Arabic numerals, its gift is poor in physical ameliora-
tion when compared to its bounty in less material
things. For theology and for architecture the world
has never seen its equal. It gave us algebra and harmony. It laid the foundation of our notion of symbolism, of chivalry, of amatory poetry, and of romantic fiction. It developed the city, it devised the
town corporation and municipal government. It
established the great feudal system which so long
ruled civilization and whose impress has remained,

even to our time, on the society of such advanced
countries as England and Prussia.

I have declared that the coming six-hundredth
anniversary of Dante's death is a memorable event
for all the nations. The great Florentine is, indeed,
a world figure. In the eyes of the universe of letters
he is a supreme and eternal representative of much
that men esteem highest — of love, of righteous
judgment, of religion voiced in poetry. For sheer
beauty, for grandiose imagination, for sweetness of
concept and phrase, he has in all time no rival but
Shakspere. Yet, despite these universal qualities, he
remains a man of his era, the interpreter, the sage,
the prophet of the Middle Ages. Medieval is all his
background, medieval his concerns, his ideas, his
life. Medieval is the material he uses, the stuff — be
it earth or hell or heaven — which his genius trans-
mutes into timeless gold. In him and in him alone
the vast formative period between Charlemagne and
Petrarch finds its complete expression. Partially expressed in the Gothic cathedral, partially in the
great schoolmen, partially in the French epic and
the Provençal lyric, partially in the Crusades, partially in feudalism, partially in the growth of bor-
oughs and trade unions, partially in the development
of nationalities, partially in the long strife of Guelfs
and Ghibellines, the age becomes fully articulate
only in the *Divine Comedy*. No other man — not
Shakspere, not Cervantes, not Goethe, not even

Homer — has ever so adequately epitomized the society of which he was a member.

Universal as he was, medieval as he was, Dante stands out as distinctly Italian. To be sure, the spirit of the Middle Ages was international, European, to a degree never since attained. One religion, one learned language, one standard united the peoples of Europe. Nevertheless, we cannot conceive of a Dante produced by any other land than Italy. Only the alliance of unbroken ancient culture with a vigorous new civilization, only the union of municipal pride and broad outlook, only the combination of a stern, bitter, strenuous life with surroundings ever beautiful, could have made such a poet, burgher and cosmopolitan, strong, severe, incisive, compact, yet infinitely tender and sweet.

This the Italians have always recognized. Diverse in habits and temperament, often hostile to one another, they are bound together by their love of Dante. Their national feeling finds a focus in him. France has her Alliance Française, Italy has her Dante Alighieri. The English-speaking nations reverence Shakspere, the Germans for a century almost made a god of Goethe, the French delight in Molière, the Spanish never tire of Cervantes, but none of these sums up the national pride and aspirations of a whole people as Dante does for the Italians. And his preëminence is not due to a paucity of great artists. Italian literature is one of the richest, her art is unsurpassed in its variety and splendor. Yet Dante, towering over all the rest, uplifted high above differences of taste and character, rises into the realm of the eternally beautiful. In selecting him as their national champion, as the ideal Italian type, his countrymen have made a noble choice.

II

Not only in a general, but in a very special sense is Dante the father of his country. Nations are held together by community of interest, by community of sentiment, by community of language. Two of these bonds are in great measure the gift of Dante. He is the chosen representative pattern, the national genius, the centre of patriotism; but he is also the founder of the Italian idiom. Before him there was no Italian language, after him there was one.

Until the thirteenth century those Italians who could write at all habitually wrote in Latin. It was to them, as it is to us, an alien tongue, artificially acquired, not spoken save in church or school; yet it was the only language they had learned to write. Some wrote it well, according to the medieval standard; many more wrote it very ill, sometimes lapsing into modern words or phrases, not infrequently making themselves quite unintelligible. An occasional poet versified in the foreign tongue of southern France. From time to time a little text was composed entirely in the despised native vernacular.

What was this vernacular? It differed according to the locality much as the most popular speech of Italy varies to-day. Not quite to the same extent, however; for the countless local dialects have for centuries been growing further and further apart. At certain great centres, where cultivated men from diverse regions were gathered together, there was a tendency to develop, by mutual compromise and by approximation to Latin, a more nearly uniform means of communication. One such centre was the court of the mighty emperor, Frederick II; another, in all probability, was the famous university of Bologna. It was doubtless this tendency, conscious or unconscious, which led Dante to believe that behind all the dialects there lurked a common ideal, a noble, fundamental mode of Italian speech, inherent in the language of every town, but peculiar to none, and never, before his day, brought to full realization. Such a language he undertook to develop, assuming as a basis the strong, rich, vivid idiom of his native Florence. After him came Petrarch and Boccaccio, using a tongue essentially the same as his; later the Medici and their followers; and the influence of such a succession of masters was so potent as to establish eventually this language, the language of Dante, as the literary medium of all Italy.

Every civilized country, in our day, has a standard speech, originally a local dialect more or less modified and gradually spread abroad, until it has become fairly uniform among the educated of all the land. In some countries it has nearly or quite supplanted its sister provincial dialects; in others it exists side by side with them. Fortunately Italy, while thus acquiring a common Italian idiom, has kept her picturesque dialects as well, and often uses them effectively in delightful literature of the more popular kind. Now, in most countries — in France, in England, in Spain, for instance — the elevation of one particular dialect into a national language has been due to political causes. Generally the choice has been determined by the seat of power, the residence of the king and his court. It is characteristic of Italy that her preference has been dictated, not by politics, but by art. No temporal authority, but the eternal authority of beauty created the Italian language and imposed it upon the whole Italian people, long before there was an Italian nation.

In literature as well as in language, Dante, with Petrarch and Boccaccio, exercised a powerful centralizing influence. The earliest vernacular literary composition in the peninsula used as its medium Provençal, the speech of southern France, where had grown up a school of amatory poetry famous throughout Europe. From northern France, where taste had run to narrative, were brought versified tales, which traveling French minstrels recited in Venetia, adapting them to their audience by an infusion of Venetian words, whence arose a fashion of constructing new epics on the old subjects, in a mixture of French and Venetian. Thus originally came to Italy those themes which, redacted in popular prose by Andrea da Barberino, reached their complete fruition in the poetry of Pulci, Boiardo, and Ariosto. French influence is doubtless to be seen also in the extensive production of didactic and satirical verse in Lombard dialect. Native, on the other hand, is the poetry resulting from the religious upheaval in Umbria, a poetry of processional songs called lauds, which, assuming a dialogue form and being performed indoors, led to the earliest type of Italian drama.

Meanwhile, at the court of Frederick II, — the most brilliant and learned court of Europe, — there arose in the second quarter of the thirteenth century a fashion of writing songs in general imitation of the Provençal style, but dressed in an Italian vernacular — a composite, changing, unformed language, which stopped short of development into a national idiom. The poets (known as the Sicilian School) were in the main the leading jurists, generals, and statesmen of the day, including the Emperor himself. With his death, in 1250, this fashion passed away, and the seat of vernacular song was shifted to Tuscany and Bologna. The early Tuscan artists, devotees of metrical and conceptual intricacy, were imitators both of the Sicilians and of the Provençal lyricists of the decline; they were decadents rather than initiators. Among the Bolognesi, however, there presently arose with Guido Guinizelli a fresh impulse — a sincerity of purpose, an elegance of style, a new idea of love, exalted and mystical. Here we find the beginning of that "dolce stil nuovo" which in Florence in the next generation was cultivated with such wondrous success by Dante and his friends. In the writings of this little group, and especially in the work of Dante himself, we first discover a medium fit to become a national language, a literature worthy to represent a nation.

III

Community of language and community of sentiment — two of the three strong ties of nationalism — are in Italy indissolubly connected with Dante. When to these was added, in the nineteenth century, community of interest, Italy became a nation. And the common interest that united the dismembered country — shattered and fragmentary since the fall of the Roman Empire — was a common desire for justice. Freedom with peace under the wing of justice became the common ideal of the people, as it had been from early times the dream of poets. The heroic war of independence was a revolt against tyrannical injustice. Love of America, so long a powerful impulse in Italian hearts, has been due partly to sympathy with us in our earlier struggle for independence, partly to an idealized conception of America as a land where justice fosters peace and liberty. In the recent World War, the Italian people, ignorant of the bargains of statesmen, was stirred to willing participation by its sense of justice outraged by the invasion of Belgium.

In Dante the strongest desire, next to the craving eternal peace and freedom of the soul in harmony with God, was a longing for justice on earth. Once and again he is on the verge of impatience with the Almighty for his apparent failure to punish iniquity. Castigation of the unrighteous constitutes the most vigorous part of the *Divine Comedy:* not only does it pervade hell where it naturally belongs; it even penetrates heaven, it reëchoes among the blest. The thought of earthly wickedness turns St. Peter's white effulgence red with wrath, and lends a bitter tang to the last words spoken by the most gentle Beatrice.

Thus does Dante represent, in a way, the third bond of nationality. He is, among poets, the great advocate of justice — justice, which, according to him, is to be attained by organization, by recognition of an international or supernational authority, and by the separation of the spiritual from the temporal power. It is God's intention (so he believed) that church and state shall rule in different spheres, one heavenly, the other worldly. In mundane affairs, above all the peoples there must be one great arbiter, one judicial administrator, who, beyond the

temptation of greed or envy, shall hold in check the
greed and envy of men and nations. Such was Dante's ideal, a theory natural enough in an age when
nationalism was in its infancy; a theory, too, which
is not without resemblance to the political ideals of
to-day. For him, however, the supreme international authority is to be, not a new creation of the
nations themselves, but an old, divinely ordained
power imposed upon them, the continued power of
the Roman Empire. The need of this authority, for
the peace of the world and for the development
of the individual, Dante argues on general prin-
ciples; the predestined right of the Roman Empire
to exercise it, he deduces from the miraculous course
of Roman history.

Dante is not merely a political theorist and an
eloquent denouncer of iniquity: he is also a prophet
of justice. Despite his own grievances, despite the
strife and cruelty of his country, he kept alive an
unwavering confidence in the ultimate triumph of
right. Again and again he sturdily affirms his belief,
investing his message with all the mysterious solem-
nity of a Revelation. A Hound shall come and drive
the Wolf back into hell, whence envy first released
it; the heavens shall roar so loud that stem shall be
turned to stern, and the fleet shall sail straight; the
noble adventure prematurely attempted by Henry
VII, the task of righting crooked Italy, shall ere long
be brought to a successful issue; soon the propitious

stars shall send to the imperial throne an avenging
Five Hundred and Ten and Five. Such forecasts he
makes with absolute conviction. In temporal justice
his faith seems to be as firm as in justice eternal.

Of the latter he treats at length in his *Paradiso*.
To call any part of the divine plan unjust, he says,
is a contradiction of terms, because what we call
justice is naught else than God's will; and of this
identity our conscience assures us, else we should
not be so profoundly shocked at an instance of apparent injustice in God's treatment of man. His
justice may pass our understanding, but He can
never be unjust. For Alighieri, life held no greater
satisfaction than the contemplation of heavenly
equity and the expectation of its fulfilment on earth.

But why is Dante's lesson so appealing? Others
have preached the same doctrine, with little effect.
The reason is clear. A supreme master of art and an
unconscious worshiper of beauty, our poet has conveyed his message in terms of irresistible charm. If
even the sternest northern nations cannot withstand
his magic, how utterly must it enthrall the beauty-
loving Italian! That Italians are beauty-lovers
needs no proof, even for the American who has never
left his native shores. Evidence abounds in their
speech, their song, their dress, their customs —
which, we may hope, no process of "Americaniza-
tion" will ever destroy. Watch the Art Museum on
a holiday, and see what people throng its halls. Go

to the opera, and look, for real appreciation of sweet
music, at the gallery crowded with Italians. In
what other country is literature in the grand style
enjoyed even by the most illiterate? What unlettered man but an Italian could listen with rapture,
though quite incapable of following the thought, to
the mere melody of Dante's verse, and never have
enough? Where else is such honor paid to the "bello
stile"? It was indeed a fitting act of divine justice
to bestow the most beautiful of poets upon the
people that is fondest of beauty.

Chapter IV

ILLUMINATION

I

O immaginativa, che ne rube
    Tal volta sì di fuor ch' uom non s' accorge
    Perchè d' intorno suonin mille tube,
Chi move te, se il senso non ti porge?
    Moveti lume che nel ciel s' informa
    Per sè o per voler che giù lo scorge?
                           [*Purg.*, XVII, 13–18.]

WAS Dante inspired — not in the figurative, literary way, as when we call Shakspere or Goethe an inspired poet; but really filled with the breath of the Lord, and speaking his message, as spake Moses, David, and Paul? The distinction between intellectual and divine illumination, though often blurred by the sophistry of unavowed skepticism, is clear enough to a clear-thinking mind, and was clearly recognized by Dante.

At the outset of his *Inferno* this Dante appeals to the Muses, who, as he has explained in his *Vita Nuova* (chap. xxv), are merely a poetic personification of the poet's art:

O Muses, soaring genius, aid me now!
                           [*Inf.*, II, 7.]

Again, on the threshold of his *Purgatorio* he appeals to the same power:

> But now let buried poesy arise,
> O sacred Muses! Yours alone am I.
> Calliope, draw nearer to the skies!
>
> [*Purg.*, I, 7–9.]

Calliope, leader of the Muses, inspirer of epic verse, patroness of style and elocution, had long since been thus invoked by Virgil, Dante's master:

> Thee I beseech, Calliope: breathe on the soul of the singer!
>
> [*Æneid*, IX, 525.]

But the song of Heaven, the *Paradiso*, calls higher for help:

> O good Apollo, fill me with thy power
> For this concluding work, that I may get
> Deservingly the precious laurel dower!
> One peak of old Parnassus hath as yet
> Sufficed for me, but now I need them both
> To meet the crowning task that still is set.
>
> [*Par.*, I, 13–18.]

Two summits, or two ridges, cap the mountain of song, as Lucan and Lucian tell us. One of these Dante assigns as a dwelling to the Muses, or human art; the other to Apollo, or art divine. For his last voyage the bold traveler needs every guidance, earthly and heavenly: godlike wisdom must fill his sails, godlike artistry must stand at the helm, while sage Poetics shall chart his course by the stars:

> The sea I sail was never sailed before.
> Minerva breathes, Apollo guides my ship;
> And Muses nine the northern stars explore.
>
> [*Par.*, II, 7–9.]

Now, in one sense, all products of the talent of man are of divine origin; for every human soul, ere the body is born, is created by God, with its special powers of insight and comprehension; and every human mind is shaped by the stars that preside over its nativity, these stars being the instruments of the angels, God's ministers, who execute his eternal plan.

> The spheres of nature, stamping their impress
>   On mortal wax, without respect to place
>   Or person, rightly do their business.
>   [*Par.*, VIII, 127–129.]

When Dante, in his journey through the heavens, reaches the last visible sphere, the sphere of the fixed stars, he there enters his native constellation of Gemini, source of learning and literary skill:

> O glorious stars, which teem eternally
>   With mighty power, O light to which I owe
>   My genius, wholly, such as it may be,
> With you arose the sun and went below
>   (The sun, progenitor of mortal life),
>   When first I felt the Tuscan breezes blow.
>   [*Par.*, XXII, 112–117.]

Both nature and divine grace had favored Dante: the stars had given him talent, God had given him vision. As Beatrice declares:

> Thanks to the whirl of giant wheels on high,
>   Which every seed to this or that incline
>   According to the stars that fill the sky, —
> And thanks to bounteous dower of grace divine,

Which rains from clouds so far from mortal view
Mine eyes shall ne'er behold them, nor shall thine,—
This man had in him, when his life was new,
    Such potency that every gladsome gift
    Might well have proved in him its promise true.
                                        [*Purg.*, xxx, 109–117.]

But the use we make of our qualities depends on ourselves. Whether our acts and words be good or evil, whether the seed implanted in us shall ripen to sweet or bitter fruit, the merit or the guilt is our own; for we have conscience and free will. If we fail, the stars are not to blame.

Subject in freedom to a mightier Soul
    A higher Nature, ye derive from it
    Intelligence, beyond the stars' control.
                                        [*Purg.*, xvi, 79–81.]

It follows that the poet's utterances, drawn from his special range of vision, fashioned by his free choice, can base no claim to inspiration on the God-given wit without which they never could have been. They are the words of the individual man, not of his Maker.

Real inspiration is something quite different: it is the voice of God dictating a message, which the prophet receives and delivers. This voice, this light have in the past come to many, even to some who were outside the fold. Theologians early recognized that those ancient Greek philosophers whose doctrines are so strangely akin to Christian teaching may have been partially illumined by a miracle of

grace. To a like wonder the Sibyls may have owed
their supernatural gift of prophecy. One may even
be an inspired prophet unawares, as was Virgil when
he wrote his Fourth Eclogue.

> Thou didst as one who fareth forth by night
>> With lantern held behind, which helps not him,
>> But after him the people leads aright.
>>> [*Purg.*, xxii, 67–69.]

In Dante's Limbus, whose dark air is a-quiver
with longing eternally unfulfilled, the abode of virtuous heathen and unbaptized children, stands a
Noble Castle brightly illuminated; there dwell the
great sages and heroes who, knowing not the true
faith, received nevertheless some measure of divine
enlightenment.

> The honorable fame reëchoing
>> And heralding their names to mortal ears
>> Wins grace in Heaven, and such reward doth bring.
>>> [*Inf.*, iv, 76–78.]

By the most famous of the illumined poets of old,
Dante is received as a fellow. With Virgil at his
side, he meets Homer, Horace, Ovid, and Lucan.

> They spake together for a little while,
>> Then turned to me with hospitable hand;
>> My master watched their welcome with a smile.
> Still more they did — an honor great and grand!
>> For they received me in their company,
>> And I was sixth in that enlightened band.
>>> [*Inf.*, iv, 97–102.]

Dante, who was no fool, knew well enough that he was a fit companion for the finest singers of antiquity; he knew well enough that since ancient Greece and Rome no one had sung as he did; and he knew also that he could sing of sacred things beyond the reach of any other poet, ancient or modern.

> O ye who, following in little boats,
>   Eager to listen, have been led away
>   Behind my ship, which singeth as it floats,
> Go back and seek your shores while yet ye may!
>   Tempt not the main; for, losing sight of me,
>   Ye haply on the deep were left astray.
>
> *[Par.*, II, 1–6.]

Did he ever ask himself, I wonder, whether it could be that the breath of the Lord had breathed upon him, whether some remnant of the grace bestowed on the Hebrew prophets — even upon pagan philosophers and poets — had descended upon him? Would such a thought have been presumptuous?

Dante was on his guard against presumption; he recognized pride as his besetting sin. How sympathetically he depicts those sinners whose downfall was due to pride of intellect, to misuse of a special gift of nature and grace! Imperishable is the image of Farinata, the haughty heretic,

> Standing aloft with breast and brow erect,
>   As held he Hell in fathomless contempt.
>
> *[Inf.*, x, 35–36.]

To the mystic seer, Joachim of Calabria, whose prophetic flights were sometimes of dubious ortho-

doxy, and to the audacious philosopher, Sigier of
Brabant, whose orthodoxy, in one important matter,
was worse than doubtful, he assigns a place in
Heaven, among the lights of theology. Unforgettable is the poet's pity as he gazes on the distorted
forms of the magicians and soothsayers, another
class of beings exceptionally endowed:

> Think, reader, for thyself, so God allow
>   Thee profit from thy reading, think, I say,
>   How I could keep mine eyes unmoistened now.
>
> .   .   .   .
>
> Indeed I wept, against a boulder prest
>   That edged the rocky ridge, until my guide
>   Exclaimed: "Art still as foolish as the rest?"
>   [*Inf.*, xx, 19–21, 25–27.]

Presently return to memory, flame-enveloped, the
evil counselors, entrusted with the perilous gift of
eloquence, among them the indomitable Ulysses,
most romantic of all figures in the *Divine Comedy*.

> Then sorrowed I, and sorrow now again,
>   When I recall the sight that grieves me still;
>   And more than ever I my wit restrain
> Nor let it run without the check of will,
>   Lest whatsoever good a friendly star
>   Or something higher hath given, I turn to ill.
>   [*Inf.*, xxvi, 19–24.]

And we know that he succeeded. Ere the end, he
had subdued pride, we know: for, on high, Beatrice
avers that her disciple possesses hope, the certain
expectation of future blessedness (*Paradiso*, xxv,

52–54); and he has already been assured (*Paradiso*, x, 87) that no man once admitted to Paradise descends to earth without promise of return. Vainglory he has banished, at least from his great poem. However he may have longed to be the recipient of a divine mission, he never proclaims himself a mouthpiece of God. For grace to make the most of his own uncommon aptitude he ardently prayed; and if from time to time he wondered whether any of the heavenly words that sprang to his lips were whispered from above, he let drop no hint of it, save perhaps in the little passage, *ond'io principio piglio:*

> Imagination, which dost often steal
> The outer world from us, and not a shrill
> Is heard, tho' close a thousand trumpets peal,
> Who wakes thee, if the senses all are still?
> Wakes thee a light engendered in the stars
> Spontaneously, or by directing Will?
>
> [*Purg.*, XVII, 13–18.]

II

> O vero isfavillar del santo spiro!
> Come si fece subito e candente
> Agli occhi miei, che vinti non soffriro!
>
> [*Par.*, XIV, 76–78.]

Of inner illumination, the inspiration of inborn genius, Dante had no lack and no doubt. I shall not now discourse of his skill as a craftsman: let us dismiss the Muses of poetry and look to Apollo, leader of the spirit. Considered as a spiritual guide, Dante may be called a mystic realist. His peculiar talent lies in the transmutation of closely observed real phenomena into mystic message. The material facts of life he clearly sees, and confronts them sturdily as facts; but he discerns in them a supersensual significance, an allegorical, moral, anagogical meaning. Thus the book of life, without ceasing to be a true story, becomes a volume of symbols. In its double function, life is like the Bible, as seen by its symbolist expositors. Not the Bible alone, but also the *Iliad* used to be so expounded; likewise the *Æneid*, the *Metamorphoses*, and other masterpieces.

For Dante, then, the world is full of hidden teachings, which it is his business to discover and impart. Cato and Martia, for instance, were historical people, who had a literal existence, but their career contained a cryptic lesson unsuspected by themselves; for the return of Martia to her first husband, Cato, after the death of Hortensius, is a symbol of the reversion of the noble human soul to God in old age. Even so in our own lives, and in the lives of those about us, lurk mystic meanings visible to those who have eyes to see.

Once, in his youth, Dante wrote for his friend, Guido Cavalcanti, a dainty compliment to two damsels, in the form of a sonnet. Out of courtesy to the recipient he naturally put the name of Guido's sweetheart before that of his own. In later years, when he was reëditing this sonnet and meditating over it, he detected in the order of the names a

mysterious correspondence with the facts: for, on
the occasion which gave rise to the poem, the first-
mentioned young lady, whose name was Joan, had
walked a little ahead of the second mentioned, Mistress Bice, even as her masculine namesake, John
the Baptist, had preceded Christ. The first maiden
had indeed been named Joan simply because she
was predestined to walk before Beatrice on this particular momentous occasion.

In events seemingly trivial may lie a solemn por-
tent. I have ventured to guess that the mysterious
number nine, which (as the square of the Trinity)
is conceived by the author to represent a miracle,
and which persistently haunts the relations of Beatrice to Dante through the prose exegesis of the
New Life, originated in the apparent chance that
impelled our poet to give Bice the ninth place in a
boyish versified enumeration of the sixty most
beautiful ladies of Florence.

Now let us consider one striking but typical example of the poet's illumination, his gift of trans-
forming real experience into spiritual symbolism.
Two circumstances of Dante's life brought him into
close affinity with St. Paul. One was his attempt to
visualize the glories of Heaven, an effort to transport
himself thither in imagination, following Beatrice,
who had been taken from earth. "I knew a man,"
says St. Paul (II Corinthians, xii, 2–4), ". . . how
that he was caught up into paradise, and heard un-

speakable words, which it is not lawful for a man to utter." This rapture he does not relate, because, he declares, "it is not expedient for me doubtless to glory." Likewise Dante, excusing himself for his failure to narrate the passing of his most gentle lady, alleges that "it is not meet for me to treat thereof, inasmuch as in such treatment I must needs be a praiser of myself, which is altogether unmeet and blameworthy in him who does it" (*Vita Nuova*, chap. xxix). Afterwards, indeed, he did publish his maturer vision in the *Divine Comedy;* for self-praise is justifiable "when from discourse of one's self very great utility to others ensues by way of instruction; which reason moved Augustine in his *Confessions* to speak of himself" (*Convivio*, I, ii). On his heavenly journey Dante knows not whether he was nothing but soul, the last created part of man, or soul and body together:

> Whether alone that part of me was I
> Which thou, Heaven-ruling Love, didst last create,
> Thou know'st, whose splendor lifted me on high.
> [*Par.*, I, 73–75.]

The same doubt was in the mind of St. Paul: "whether in the body, or out of the body, I cannot tell: God knoweth."

The other common experience was a temporary loss of sight, an affliction that miraculously befell Saul on his way to Damascus, as is related in Acts ix, 3–18: "And as he journeyed, he came near

Damascus, and suddenly there shined round about him a light from heaven: and he fell to the earth. . . . And Saul arose from the earth; and when his eyes were opened, he saw no man: but they led him by the hand, and brought him into Damascus. And he was there three days without sight, and neither did eat nor drink." During these days, it was believed, he had his vision of Paradise. Dante's blinding, as told in the *Convivio*, III, ix, was neither total nor supernatural: "Greatly wearying my eyes with assiduous reading, I so weakened my powers of sight that the stars looked to me clouded, all of them, by a sort of white blur. By long rest in dark, cool places, and by cooling the ball of the eye with pure water, I fixed once more the scattered faculty and recovered my former good condition of sight." In the *Vita Nuova* (chap. XI) Dante poetically attributes another like mishap, not to study, but to assiduous weeping: "By this rekindling of sighs was rekindled my assuaged tearfulness to such a degree that mine eyes looked like two things whose only desire was to weep; and by long continuance of weeping there came around them a purple color, such as often appears from suffering of some kind."

> Mine eyes are vanquisht, and have lost the strength
> To look at one who may return their gaze.
> [*Vita Nuova*, Sonnet XXIII.]

In these accounts, indeed, there is no suggestion of a similarity to the blinding of Saul, who for a brief

time lost his earthly sight that his spiritual vision
might be brighter. It is only when the poet turns
his physical accident to account in providing detail
for religious symbolism that his case becomes parallel to that of St. Paul. In the allegory of Paradise,
Dante, too, is blinded that he may see the clearer;
during the unseeing interval, the doctrine of love is
expounded. The blindness has come without warning:

> What consternation set my soul astir,
>   When, turning to contemplate Beatrice,
>   I could not see her more, tho' close to her
> I still remained, and in the world of bliss!
> > [*Par.*, xxv, 136–139.]

His sight has been quenched by a glowing flame (the
effulgence of St. John, exponent of love), into which
he has intently gazed; not until he turns about to
look at other things does he become aware, to his
amazement, that he is blind. Presently he sees
again, and better; but still not well enough. Once
more, on entering the Empyrean, the real Heaven
of spirit, Dante's vision is clarified by momentary
extinction:

> Thus round about me shined a living light
>   Which left me covered o'er with such a veil
>   Of brilliancy that nothing met my sight.
> > [*Par.*, xxx, 49–51.]

Again and again, in the *Purgatorio* and in the
Paradiso, we find the poet blinded or dazzled by an
intense light.

> As now to us the bird of Heaven did fare,
>   The nearer he, the brighter did he shine;
>   And when he came, 't was more than eye could bear.
>   [*Purg.*, ii, 37–39.]

The dazzling objects in Purgatory are angels, ministers of divine illumination.

> The sight of him had snatcht mine eyes away;
>   And I fell in behind my leaders twain,
>   Like one who walks by ear as best he may.
>   [*Purg.*, xxiv, 142–144.]

One angel, hidden in its own light, sings a greeting.

> We heard within a light that stood aglow:
>   "Venite, benedicti Patris mei."
>   I could not look, it overcame me so.
>   [*Purg.*, xxvii, 58–60.]

Another, with a face of unbearable brilliancy, holds in his hand a naked sword,

> Toward us reflecting all its rays so keen
>   That more than once I vainly turned my eyes.
>   [*Purg.*, ix, 83–84.]

In Paradise, whose tenuous fabric is chiefly light and music, the dazzling is of course more frequent. The effulgence may proceed from a saint,

> So fiery sharp it overwhelmed my sight.
>   [*Par.*, xxv, 27.]

It may shine from Beatrice:

> She flasht upon my turning eye so quick
>   My sense at first could not endure the strain.
>   [*Par.*, iii, 128–129.]

Again it emanates from Christ:

> And thro' the living sheen came shining bright
> The gleaming Substance, with such clarity
> Mine eye, which saw, could not endure the sight.
> [*Par.*, xxiii, 31–33.]

Sometimes, in Dante's fancy, the blinding object is the sun:

> As sunshine bows the eyes with heaviness
> And veils itself with brightness overdone,
> My strength was now unequal to the stress.
> [*Purg.*, xvii, 52–54.]

Noteworthy is this realistic touch — the sensation of weight over the brows. It occurs again:

> Mid-nose exactly fell the solar rays, —
> For round the mountain we had circled so
> That we were facing straight the sunset blaze, —
> When, worse than I had felt in all the glow,
> A heaviness descended on my brow,
> Amazing me, because I did not know.
> [*Purg.*, xv, 7–12.]

What Dante did not know is that the sudden increase of light, with its effect of weight, was due to the approach of a shining angel. On another occasion the crushing light comes from two of the Disciples, Peter and James, whom Dante metaphorically designates as the hills unto which he lifts up his eyes:

> Thus comforts me St. Peter's flaming mate;
> Wherefore I lift mine eyes unto the hills,
> Which erst had bowed them with excessive weight.
> [*Par.*, xxv, 37–39.]

The inadequacy of the human eye to bear the
direct light of the sun is a familiar thought to Dante.

> As sunshine in the eye that quivers most.
> [*Par.*, xxx, 25.]

In the *Vita Nuova* (chap. XLII) he says: "Our intellect is to those blessed souls as our feeble eye is to
the sun." And in the second *canzone* of the *Convivio*,
vv. 59–60:

> These things our understanding overpower,
> E'en as a ray of sun a fragile eye.

A symbolic sun is no less overpowering:

> O kindly Power, that shapest with thy light,
>   Thou didst depart aloft to spare mine eyes,
>   Whose strength did not suffice for such a sight.
> [*Par.*, xxiii, 85–87.]

As we have noted, the glory of the angels, God's
ministers, is beyond human vision:

> Mine eyes discerned aright each golden tress,
>   But could not rightly see the shining face —
>   Like any power confounded by excess.
> [*Purg.*, viii, 34–36.]

In these passages we have encountered sundry
details remarkable for their verity: the blurring of
the sight, the sense of oppression just above the
brows, the inclination to bend the eyes down, the
sudden terror that is felt on looking about and finding one's self blinded. Another touch, still more

intimate, occurs in the last canto of the poem: the feeling that, having once mastered the fearful brilliancy and fixed one's eyes on the light, it is useless to turn elsewhere:

> So sharply cut mine eyes the living ray,
>   I think that I had nothing seen at all,
>   If I from it my sight had turned away.
>
> [*Par.*, XXXIII, 76–78.]

Where did Dante get this knowledge? We are sure that he was an adept in astronomy; we are almost certain that he performed an experiment in optics with a light and three mirrors (*Paradiso*, II, 94–105); we are amazed at the accuracy with which he could describe the course of the sun (*Convivio*, III, v). In *Convivio*, II, x, he shows a pretty clear understanding of the mechanism of sight. The *Divine Comedy*, too, contains a couple of arresting passages which reveal study of the eye:

> A sudden glare awakens us from sleep,
>   With sense of sight intent to meet the gleam
>   Which membrane after membrance pierces deep.
>
> [*Par.*, XXVI, 70–72.]

The second one is still more curious in its portrayal of the same phenomenon, regarded from the standpoint of consciousness:

> When all at once a sudden flash of light
>   On sleeping eyes doth knock, our slumber breaks,
>   But, broken, quivers ere it perish quite.
>
> [*Purg.*, XVII, 40–42.]

It is natural to connect Dante's interest in the eye
and the phenomena of sight with the passing infirmity whereof mention has been made.   He was inevitably concerned with sight because his sight had
been marred and threatened.   Is it over-bold on our
part to conjecture a more special experience than the
incident he discloses? Fond star-gazer that he was,
did he ever imprudently turn his gaze on the sun?
In his allegory, at least, he did so, while standing in
the Garden of Eden beside Beatrice, who set the
example:

> In quick response I did what she had done,
>   When I had caught the image of her act:
>   Beyond our wont I stared into the sun.
> Much strength is there which human sense hath lackt
>   Since Adam fell; because that favored spot
>   Was made for man when man was still intact.
> I could not bear it long; but yielded not
>   Until I saw it sparkle all around
>   Like iron drawn from furnace boiling hot.
> Then suddenly was day to daylight bound
>   (So it appeared), as if the One who Can
>   A second sun to deck the sky had found.
>   [*Par.*, 1, 52–63.]

If without glorying it is meet for me to speak of
myself, it so happens that I am able to verify the
accuracy of Dante's observations; for once, in a
moment of rashness, I stared at the sun. It was on
October 20, 1892, when a partial eclipse was observ-
able in Boston. I had forgotten the impending
event; but suddenly noticing the diminution of light,

I thoughtlessly looked up, and then, being in a quiet
street, fascinated as it were by curiosity, I kept my
eyes fixed on the waning orb. The first sensation
was painful: a dizziness, a heaviness over the brows,
an almost irresistible pressure to lower the eyes.
Presently, however, these symptoms passed away,
and I was able to look steadily without the least dis-
comfort, even with a certain sense of exhilaration,
but with a vague misgiving that it would not do to
avert my gaze. What surprised me most was that
light and dark were transposed, the obscured section
of the disk showing a luminous gray, the unshaded
part nearly black. After watching the strange sight
for some time with satisfaction, I turned to walk
home, and discovered, to my chagrin, that I could
hardly see. As Dante says,

> That temporary impotence to see
>   Which blinds an eye just striken by the sun
>   All sightless for the moment rendered me.
> [*Purg.*, xxxii, 10-12.]

All was dim; barely could I find my way. Some
days of rest and darkness were needed to restore my
sight; for weeks I could not discern the letters on a
printed page; and for months afterward I could not
endure anything white or shining. Instinctively I
avoided persons wearing white garments. Once, in
the sunshine, I suddenly encountered an old gen-
tleman with long white hair and beard, whose glare
upset me for a good bit. Dante's angels always

make me think of him. Oddly enough, I was so
ashamed of my folly that I confessed it only to
my oculist and two or three others; and to this day
I have told it to very few. Most people thought
that my brief disability was caused by overstudy.

Now let us return to the passage that narrates
Dante's misadventure (*Convivio*, III, ix): "Such an
appearance may be due also to the organ of sight,
namely the eye, which by sickness or fatigue is affected by some particular coloring or enfeeblement.
It often happens, for example, that when the coat
of the pupil is reddened by the corruption of some
infirmity, things almost all look ruddy; and so the
stars appear colored. When sight is enfeebled, too,
there occurs a certain scattering of sense, so that
things do not appear united but scattered, very
nearly as our writing looks on damp paper. That is
why many people, when they read, hold the writ far
enough away from their eyes for the image to reach
them more easily and sharply, and thereby the
letter becomes clearer to their sight. For this reason
even the stars may appear murky. Whereof I had
experience the very year in which this poem [*Convivio*, Canzone 2] came into the world; for greatly
wearying my eyes with assiduous reading, I so
weakened my powers of sight that the stars looked
to me clouded, all of them, by a sort of white blur.
By long rest in dark, cool places, and by cooling the
ball of the eye with pure water, I fixed once more

the scattered faculty and recovered my former good condition of sight."

The poem in question, *Amor che nella mente mi ragiona*, was composed after the first *canzone* of the *Convivio*, namely *Voi che intendendo il terzo ciel movete*, which, in turn, being cited in the *Paradiso* (VIII, 37) by the young prince Carlo Martello, must have been written before his death in 1295, and probably saw the light not long before his visit to Florence in the spring of 1294. Our poem, then, *Amor che nella mente mi ragiona*, would doubtless fall somewhere in 1295; and that would be the year in which Dante's sight was impaired. Now, it appears that on December 8, 1295, there was a partial eclipse of the sun, visible in Italy. At this point let us recall a significant reference to a partial eclipse in the *Divine Comedy*. The word "eclipse" occurs in two other places, but in neither has it the appositeness it has in this passage, wherein Dante is seen trying to penetrate with his eyes the light that envelops St. John:

> As one who stares and strives with all his might
>   To see the sun eclipst to some degree,
>   And who by seeing robs himself of sight,
> Thus I before that latest brilliancy;
>   Until I heard: "To see an absent thing
>   Whose place is elsewhere, why dost dazzle thee?"
>   [*Par.*, xxv, 118–123.]

If the happening I have imagined be true, — and even if it be not, even if Dante needed no eclipse to hurt his eyes, — we may see, in all that has preceded, the difference between an illumined poet and an ordinary man. What to the latter is a trivial incident, annoying, perhaps mortifying, but commonplace, is by inspired genius so transmuted that it comes to represent the refinement of vision from physical sight to mental comprehension, and from comprehension to intuition or immediate perception, until the seer shall no longer see through a glass, darkly, but face to face.

Chapter V

THE CENTRE OF THE CIRCLE

If any could desire what he is incapable of possessing, despair
must be his eternal lot. — WILLIAM BLAKE.

"I AM as the centre of a circle, to which the parts
of the circumference bear the same relation; but
thou art not thus" (*Vita Nuova*, XII). So speaks the
Spirit of Love in Dante's *New Life*, the story of the
author's psychic vicissitudes under the influence of
Beatrice, Bestower of Blessings. Love, the motive
power of earth and heaven, is in itself a type of
perfect equilibrium, even as the centre of a circle,
equally distant from all points in its circumference;
but mortals moved by love seldom preserve this
even poise, being by temperament imperfect, that
is, unbalanced.

The alternation of balance and unbalancing is the
theme of Dante's youthful autobiography. The
hero is at once a lover, seeking the highest serenity
of love, and a religious spirit, in quest of stable ad-
justment to God's will. First we see him, rapt in
admiration of an angelic maiden, stimulated to an
ecstatic exaltation that seems, but is not, a true
equilibrium — not true, because it has in it a selfish
strain, a self-love stronger than the love for the be-

loved. How many Romeos, exulting in their devotion, are really more in love with themselves than
with their Juliets!

An affection so ill-poised is no safeguard against
infidelity; and, in truth, we presently discover our
hero hovering about other damsels: first, the one
who in church happened to sit in a direct line between him and Beatrice; next, the young lady to
whom he showed so much attention, in verse and
otherwise, that "many people discoursed of it beyond the bounds of courtesy," and the most gentle
Beatrice, "destroyer of all vices and queen of virtues, on passing through a certain place, denied me
her very sweet greeting, in which all my blessedness
consisted."

Then it was that in a dream the Spirit of Love,
piteously weeping, visited his disciple, and, being
asked why he wept, replied in the words already
cited: "I am as the centre of a circle, to which the
parts of the circumference bear the same relation;
but thou art not thus." "Thereupon," says Dante,
"as I meditated over his words, it seemed to me
that he had spoken to me right darkly." So hard
it is for us to accept a diagnosis which attributes our
malady to an excess of self, disturbing the balance
of our relations. Not until his most gentle lady had
so far forgotten her gentleness as to join other ladies
in laughing at the discomfiture of her admirer at a
wedding banquet; not until a group of Beatrice's

girl friends had pointed out to the poet the discrepancy between his protestations and his practices,
did he begin to appreciate his error and resolve to
rectify it.

Henceforth the hateful *ego* is to be excluded from
his worship and banished from his verse. A period
of new serenity ensues, broken only by sympathy
with the grief of Beatrice over the death of her
father, and by a morbid fear of losing Beatrice herself — a fear that is justified by the event, at the
very moment when Dante is attaining to a state of
stable equilibrium in apparently altruistic service.
Alas! the balance was too precarious. The lover's
poise depended on the bodily presence of the Bestower of Blessings; by her death the equilibrium
was broken. As she herself says, in Dante's *Purgatory* (xxx, 124–132):

> No sooner had I reached maturity
>   And changed that life for life without an end,
>   Than he to others turned, forsaking me.
> When I from flesh to spirit did ascend,
>   And when my loveliness and goodness grew,
>   Less dear was I, less comfort could I lend.
> A truthless track he took, turning anew,
>   Chasing deceptive shapes of happiness
>   Which never keep their promise full and true.

He allows himself, though not without a struggle,
to be lured from his allegiance by the compassionate
regard of another gentle lady, who, seated at a window, has sympathetically watched his sorrow. Once

more he is startled into rectitude by a dream. This time it is not the Spirit of Love that comes to him, but Beatrice herself, fashioned and attired as she was when Dante first saw her, in her ninth year. At last he is on the way to the centre of the circle, a long, difficult way, which reaches its goal only at the close of the *Divine Comedy*. The *New Life* ends with the departure on the journey. "A wondrous vision appeared to me, wherein I saw things which made me resolve to say no more of this blessed lady until I could treat of her more fitly. To attain to this am I studying with all my might, as she verily knoweth. Therefore, if it be the pleasure of Him by whom all things live, that my life endure for some years, I hope to say of her what never yet was said of any woman. And then may He who is Lord of Kindness grant that my soul go forth to behold the glory of its Queen." (*Vita Nuova*, XLIII.)

In order to know the calm of perfect love, in order to win the peace of Heaven, the Christian lover must "study with all his might" to gain that balance of all his powers and desires which alone can make him fit for immortal praise of his lady or for eternal satisfaction hereafter. Every moral virtue, Dante declares in his *Banquet*, "every virtue which by its exercise makes men happy, is derived originally from a single root; and this root is an *elective habit* that dwells only in the middle." (*Convivio*, Canzone III.) In other words, the essence of virtue is the habit of choosing the golden mean between two vicious extremes, according to the ethical doctrine of Aristotle. The man who has this habit may be called truly noble; for nobility is the gift of neither wealth nor family — it is the direct gift of God to his elect, a privilege which lifts them from the common human state almost to the divine, investing them with godlike harmony.

Such harmony is unknown on earth to ordinary mortals; in them, wishes do not match faculties, cravings outstrip satisfactions. The absolutely perfect balance is in God alone, in whom all qualities are in exact counterpoise — an equality, says Dante, beyond all compare. But the human soul, when it comes into the presence of this primal and eternal Equality, so far participates in its equilibrium that its desires are precisely adjusted to its means of fulfilment. In Heaven there can be no discontent. With the following terse and difficult phrases Dante expresses this thought, in his *Paradise*, directing his words to the soul of his great-great-grandfather, Cacciaguida, the Crusader.

> Then I began: "In every one of you,
>   As soon as Primal Balance met your sight,
>   Did inclination balance power to do;
> Because the Sun that gave you heat and light,
>   Desire and wit, hath such an even glow
>   That every best similitude is slight.
> But mortal wish and wisdom, down below,
>   Unmated fly, uneven in their speed,
>   For reasons which ye heavenly spirits know."
>   [*Par.*, xv, 73–81.]

What a paradise our earth would be, could a like equilibrium be established here, could "inclination balance power to do"! It is a commonplace of Stoic philosophy that the contented man is he who craves only that which he can get. But the maxim may be turned about: we may say that the contented man is he who can get what he craves. We may strive for contentment by progressive abnegation, by discarding one ambition or one ideal or one convenience after another, until we finally throw away even our drinking-gourd. On the other hand, we may seek the beatifying satisfaction by increase of our powers, by so developing our capacities in every direction that any reasonable wish shall be fulfilled, and the divine balance of desire and act, the divine harmony of faculties, the divine contentment shall be approximated even here below. Such is the contentment, surely, of the soul that Dante calls "noble."

From one point of view, this perfect equipoise, with all its elements carried to infinity, is the fundamental characteristic of God; and he manifests it in his products, both in things of spirit and in things of matter. Both the everlasting universe and the world of time, a creation of his eternity, reveal the harmony of their Maker. As sin corresponds to atonement, Adam to Christ, Eve to Mary, as the prophecies of the Old Testament match the events of the New, so the human and the divine are mated in Christ, so the Holy Ghost proceeds equally from

Father and Son, so the three Persons of the Godhead — types of Power, Wisdom, and Love — have
an even share in the single act of creation.

> Looking upon His Offspring with the Love
>   Which everlastingly proceeds from each,
>   The primal, unimagined Power above
> Created all that circles in the reach
>   Of space or mind, so planfully, it must
>   Some taste of Him to every gazer teach.
>   [*Par.*, x, 1–6.]

No one who contemplates the world of spirit or the
world of matter, or any part thereof, can fail to receive some inkling of the infinite power which with
wisdom and love conceived all things according to a
vast, purposeful, harmonious plan.

Even in the events of history and the facts of
geography we may detect an underlying symmetry
— an unfolding symmetry in history, a static symmetry in geography. Not only are we confronted by
the great balance of Original Sin and Last Judgment, with the Atonement midway between; not
only do we discern a wonderfully exact correspondence between the incidents of the Old Testament
and those of the New, the latter being foreshadowed
by the former: we can trace also a relation between
the course of pagan and of Jewish history, the one
leading, stage by stage, from the fall of Troy to the
founding of Rome and ultimately to the creation of
the Roman Empire; the other proceeding from the
fall of man to the exaltation of Jerusalem, the birth

of Jesus, and the establishment of the Christian
Church. As Cæsar, the Founder of the Empire, was
betrayed by Brutus and Cassius, so Christ, the
Founder of the Church, was sold by Judas Iscariot.
The duration of the world is so calculated that on
the Judgment Day the number of Christians received in Heaven shall precisely equal the number
of the elect from the Old Church. All these intricate, mysterious, beautiful symmetries —which reveal themselves without end, one after another, as
we study more and more closely — are a proof of
divine origin; they are manifestly the product of an
Intelligence whose perfect inner harmony reflects
itself in its works.

Among the conspicuous events foreordained by
God is the founding of the two mighty orders, the
Franciscan and the Dominican, which Dante likens
to the two wheels of the chariot of the Church. To
the two founders and their works and followers
Dante devotes two cantos of his *Paradise*, the
eleventh and the twelfth. The story of St. Francis
is narrated in Heaven by the greatest of Domini-
cans, St. Thomas Aquinas; the tale of St. Dominic is
told by St. Bonaventure, greatest of the Francis-
cans. In the structure of these two cantos there
lurks a symmetry so concealed that it has only of
late years been observed, but so close as to prove
that the two must have been designed together by
the poet, bit by bit, line by line. For example, in

line 51 of canto XI the sun is described as rising due
east, in the equinoctial season; in line 51 of canto XII
the sun, at the same time of year, is setting due
west. In lines 61 to 63 of canto XI is described the
mystic marriage of Francis and Poverty; lines 61 to
63 of canto XII relate the mystic wedlock of Dominic and Faith. In his exact matching of the two
saints, Dante, for all his ecstatic admiration, seems
to do scant justice to St. Francis, who in reality
lived on such a different plane from St. Dominic.
To some critics it has appeared that Dante, the poet
of the Middle Ages, did not fully appreciate St.
Francis, the prophet of a new era. It may well be,
however, that the poet's compression of his estimate
of the gentle saint of Assisi is due, not to lack of understanding, but to his desire for perfect correspondence between the Italian and the Spanish leader;
and that this desire in turn is the fruit, not merely
of an artistic tendency, but rather of an overmaster-
ing wish to find everywhere, and especially in great
things, that symmetry which is the mark of God's
handiwork, the seal of divine authorship.

The trail of mystic correspondence may be followed even into the imaginings of the ancient heathen poets, who, despite their paganism, received
some degree of enlightenment from God's illuminat-
ing grace. While some of the false deities (such as
the Muses and Apollo) are nothing but allegorical
figures, and while others are fallen angels or demons

who have beguiled humanity, supreme Jove represents the real Divinity mistily conceived, as he
must be by those to whom he has not been fully revealed. The revolt of the proud angels and their
fall from Heaven is shadowed in the old story of the
battle of gods and giants. Of the flood, and of the
creation of man, there is a notion in Ovid.   The
state of original innocence, before Adam and Eve
sinned, becomes in mythology the Golden Age,
when the world was pure under the reign of Saturn;
and as the ancient poets wrote of Parnassus and
nectar and ambrosia, they had in mind a dim idea
of the Garden of Eden on its remote mountain-top.
By the curious, such parallelism may be pursued
much further and tracked in minute detail.

Let us turn from history and fiction to geography.
Not without significance is the spherical shape of the
earth, and the spherical shape of the entire physical
universe, which has the earth as centre or core; for
the sphere is the perfect solid figure, even as among
plane figures the circle is perfect, having no irregu-
larity and no beginning or end. For that reason the
heavenly bodies move in circles or combinations of
circles. Modern science has flattened the poles of
the earth, has transformed the circular orbits of the
planets into ellipses, has opened to footless discussion the question of the shape of the universe. The
medieval world may have been all wrong, but it had
a meaning, which has vanished from the world of

to-day. On the old round earth, three-fourths covered by water, was a balanced clover-leaf of three
continents — Asia, Europe, and Africa, one big and
two small. At the precise centre of all this land sat
Jerusalem, the sacred city; just between the centre
and the western extremity was Rome, the seat of
Empire and of Church. At the extreme west was
the mouth of the Mediterranean; at the extreme
east, the mouth of the Ganges. On the two sides of
the Equator the alternations of the seasons match
one another, but inverted, with winter in the north
when summer prevails in the south; while the sun,
which in the north temperate zone always passes to
the southward in its daily course from east to west,
in the south temperate zone passes correspondingly
to northward. Many phenomena, now so commonplace that we ignore them altogether, were to earlier
generations objects of eager curiosity, of wonder,
and of deep significance. Perhaps we have cause to
congratulate ourselves on our superior knowledge,
but the debit side weighs heavily against the credit;
for the extension of our familiarity has bred, if not
contempt, at least indifference, robbing us of the
zest of inquisitiveness, of constant conjecture, of
discovery, of admiration.

Admiration is the keynote of Dante's outgivings
on the subject of the great round universe. A man
of science and a fond sky-gazer, he loved to look
aloft — in the daytime at the birds, whose flights

and habits he observed and noted; in the nighttime
at the stars, his favorite companions. Each of the
three books of the *Divine Comedy* ends with the
word *stelle*, or "stars," the goal of his thoughts.
Even when he could not see them, they were in his
mind: he knew their positions in the heavens at any
given moment, their relations to one another, their
dispositions; and he liked to conjure them up before
his mind's eye. To his readers he gave credit for the
same predilection, as is shown by the many astronomical puzzles he sets before them, generally in the
form of a simile or a metaphor. One of his habitual
tricks, in the *Paradise*, is to begin a canto with a
celestial riddle of such sort. These problems, in his
judgment, are something more than an ingenious
diversion or a scientific exercise: they are a means of
widening our comprehension of the marvels of creation and our appreciation of the Power that made
them.

> Lift, reader, then, O lift with me thy lashes
>   And view the heavenly wheels, facing the spot
>   Where one rotation with another clashes.
>
> [*Par.*, x, 7–9.]

The object of the reader's contemplation, in this
case, is the angle at which the ecliptic, the circle of
the sun's annual revolution, crosses the equator, the
circle of its daily turn — an angle on which the
climate of our land depends, therefore its fitness for
human habitation and development; an angle, then,

which by the very degree of its acuteness bears testimony to an omniscient foresight.

> Now keep thy seat, O reader, and begin
>   To ponder on the feast in store for thee,
>   Wouldst thou be glad ere weariness set in.
> Now feed thyself (the viands ready be);
>   For every thoughtful care of mine is drawn
>   To treat the theme which now engages me.
> [*Par.*, x, 22–27.]

If one little angle, the crossing of two circles in the sky, be full of such portentous suggestion, what must be the possibilities of wonder and worship offered by the whole sphere of the universe, a universe of countless but perfectly adjusted bodies, of revolutions diverse and uniform! At the centre of Dante's world is the terrestrial globe, whose size was then only a little less than now, composed of earth and water, surrounded by a coating of air and a remoter coating of fire. About this solid, motionless globe revolve nine heavens, one encompassed by another, all transparent and tenuous, like so many successive, concentric soap-bubbles, all turning together once in twenty-four hours, but at the same time rotating independently at different rates and in different directions. The outermost of these films, being uniformly thin, is completely invisible. The next, or eighth, on the contrary, is filled with innumerable flecks, which are the fixed stars, arranged in mysterious patterns, or constellations.

Each of the remaining seven filmy heavens contains and carries with it one dense and therefore visible globe; and these globes are called "planets." Beginning with the highest, just below the fixed stars, they are: Saturn, Jupiter, Mars, the Sun, Venus, Mercury, the Moon. Every planet, and every constellation in the zodiac, or sun's course, exerts a certain influence; and the sum of all these influences is the force called "nature." But nature does not operate automatically; for the nine heavens are directed by nine orders of spiritual intelligences named "angels," ministers of God's will, which they eternally and ceaselessly discern and execute. The proper abode of the Lord and his angels, and also of the blest, is the realm of pure spirit, the Empyrean, or Heavenly Paradise, which lies outside and round about the spherical universe of matter. The divine power emanating from the Empyrean is received by the outermost of the revolving, material heavens, and there translated into motive force and passed on to the successive circling bodies, which transmit and differentiate it according to the needs of earth.

Such is the beautifully symmetrical world that Dante knew and never ceased to contemplate with wonder, a world wherein nothing is casual or useless. Thus are explained the interrelations of spirit and matter, of the single divine will and its infinitely varied manifestations in our universe. Man, a compound of spirit and matter, is made up of soul and body, temporarily parted by death because of human sin, but destined to be forever reunited after the Judgment Day. Man's acts are the products of his own free will, independent, though foreknown by his Maker. Man's inborn character is the result of the material influence of the stars upon his native disposition, and of the quality of grace bestowed by God upon his soul at its creation. In the human being, then, as in the universe at large, spirit and matter are consistently balanced. By his own free choice man earns eternal reward or eternal sorrow. Freedom is impossible without responsibility, there can be no responsibility without freedom; and for a creature free and responsible, everlasting pain is the inevitable consequence of wrongdoing unatoned, as everlasting joy is the result of persistent righteous choice.

Unerringly but often mysteriously just is the moral system that Dante recognized. Justice, like Love, is "as the centre of a circle, to which the parts of the circumference bear the same relation." But viewed from a wrong angle, or seen only in part, the perfect figure may appear distorted. Our idea of the just comes to us from our Maker; "justice," in fact, says Dante, is nothing but the name that mortals give to the divine will. To complain, then, that aught ordained by God is unjust is equivalent to declaring that justice is not justice, or that God's will is not God's will. In a world governed by a Lord all-powerful, all-wise, and all-loving, nothing can occur that shall be ultimately unjust. This is the firm foundation, the unshakable rock of Dante's faith. Hence came his courage and his power. Between our acts and our future joys or sorrows, he believed, there is unswerving correspondence; an exact balance is ordained between our sins and their punishments, between our merits and their rewards. As with the individual, so with society: if the world be wicked, it shall suffer; if it redeem itself, it shall be happy. As a basis of moral strength, neither science nor philosophy has yet invented a substitute for absolute faith in responsibility and justice.

Dante's faith was put to a severe test, not only by his own unjust exile and consequent lifelong misery, but also, and far more, by the failure and untimely death of that Emperor on whose success he had rested all his hopes of the moral regeneration of his country. The world is far wickeder than it used to be, he thought — as many have thought before and since his time; life is little else than clash of selfish interests, strife and fraud, bloodshed and oppression; nor can it improve without the guidance of a strong, wise, disinterested Imperial authority. We have seen how such a sublime central power shone upon the stricken world, while Dante was in his forties, in the person of a new Emperor, Henry VII, who, sharing Dante's idealism and Dante's political views, set forth to restore order and justice in Italy by reëstablishing a strong temporal government, a balance to the spiritual government of the Church. We have seen how the letters written by the poet in this period reveal an enthusiast in whom frantic jubilation contends with frantic impatience; such expectation as Dante cherished is in itself pathetic, because it is so far beyond all possibility of earthly fulfilment. We know that after the flush of initial success came chilling disillusionment, when Henry, the poet's hero, having met with stout resistance, presently died, his mission unfulfilled. With his failure fell Dante's feverish hope; no heavier disappointment ever came to man. Yet out of this ruin, faith arose once more, triumphant, steadfast, refusing to be crushed.

The two moods engendered by this tremendous experience, the mood of buoyant hope and the mood of faith unshaken, are reflected in the second and the third book of the *Divine Comedy*. While *Purgatory* exalts the liberty of human volition, *Paradise* proclaims the unchanging will of the Creator. Of the former the theme is man's redemption by his own effort, the righteous exercise of free will, culminating in the restoration of original purity; and the keynote is hope. Of the latter the subject is God's perfect but unfathomable plan, the mysterious way in which he moves, the shortness of human sight and the infinite depth of the Heavenly mind, the beatification of man by divine grace; the dominant note of the *Paradise* is faith, submissive and serene.

Faith, freedom, responsibility: a sturdy and wholesome creed! But the sociologist may ask, are men truly free; are they not the slaves of environment, the toys of heredity; and, if they are not free, how can they be held responsible? To this question Dante might have replied: whatever be our surroundings, we have the independent, unerring voice of conscience to tell us what is right and what is wrong; whatever be our temperament, we have power to curb it; whatever be our difficulties, we have free will to choose the strait and narrow path. For will is invincible; it can be thwarted only by its own act. As Dante says,

> Our will unwillingly is never spent,
>   But flareth upward like the torch's flame,
>   Howe'er the torch be violently bent.
>   [*Par.*, IV, 76–78.]

To be sure, rightdoing is harder for some than for others: harder for those whose lot is cast in nests of iniquity; harder for those who lack trustworthy counsel. But it is possible for all, and, being possible, is justly demanded. The harder the battle, the prouder the victory. And victory is surely his who strives at all times with all his might to be "as the centre of a circle, to which the parts of the circumference bear the same relation."

During some epochs of history, alas! the battle is all too often a losing fight, so strong is the fashion of sin, so weak is the restraint of law; and Dante's own age was one of these. In God's plan for humanity, provision is made for temporal guidance, corresponding to the spiritual direction of the Church. Only by a proper balance of the worldly and the ghostly power — so Dante believed — can righteousness be maintained. Should Empire encroach on Church, the latter would not be free to minister adequately to man's religious needs. Should Church usurp the functions of Empire, as it had done in Dante's day, — or so he thought, — it would take upon itself secular duties which it was ill adapted to perform, and would at the same time suppress the only power competent to perform them. According to Dante's political theory, which he defended with characteristic vigor, Church and State are equally ordained by God and responsible to him alone. While the Church is the more venerable, the State is the elder of the two sacred and necessary institutions, and in its field its authority is supreme; even Christ submitted to it, giving an example sadly disregarded by his successors.

In the planet Jupiter, in Dante's *Paradise*, the multitudinous souls of just princes, appearing as specks of light, flit hither and thither in flocks, like birds, and finally compose themselves in the form of a huge letter M, the initial of "Monarchy." Then, by a shift of the singing spirits, the M is transformed into a gigantic Eagle, the symbol of the Holy Roman Empire. Thus, in a glorious allegorical pageantry of lights, the poet sets forth the doctrine which, in his Latin treatise on *Monarchy*, he argues in the terse logic of prose. Justice is always and everywhere the same: as the composite Eagle speaks with one voice, so the utterances of the just form a perfect unison, with no discordant note. The embodiment of human justice is Monarchy, the State, the harmony of the just; and the State predestined to supreme secular authority is the Roman Empire, whose holy mission is proved by the miraculous course of Roman history, from the fall of Troy to the rise of Cæsar, and by Christ's submission to the government of Rome.

"In truth," says Dante in his *Banquet* (iv, iv), "the primal basis of Imperial Majesty is the need of human civilization, which is ordained for one end, namely, for happy life, to which no one is sufficient to attain without the help of another, inasmuch as man hath need of many things which a single one cannot supply. Wherefore the Philosopher declares that 'man is by nature a social creature.' And even as a man for his completeness requires the domestic company of a family, so a household for its completeness requires a neighborhood, else it would suffer many wants, which would be an obstacle to happiness. And forasmuch as a neighborhood cannot give satisfaction to itself in everything, to satisfy it there must needs be a city. Furthermore, the city needs for its industries and its protection to have intercourse and fraternity with surrounding cities; therefore was made the kingdom. Now inasmuch as the human spirit is not tranquil in a limited possession of land, but forever desires more land to acquire, as we see by experience, it must needs be that discords and wars arise between kingdom and kingdom; which wars are the plague of cities, and, through cities, of neighborhoods, and, through neighborhoods, of households, and, through households, of the individual; and thus happiness is prevented. Wherefore, to abolish these wars and their causes, it is necessary that all the earth, and all that it is given to the human race to possess, be a State, that is, a single realm with a single ruler, who, possessing everything and unable to desire more, shall keep the kings contented in the confines of their kingdoms, so that peace shall be among them; in which peace cities may be at rest, and in this rest neighborhoods may love one another, and in this love households may supply their every need, and by this supply man may live happily; which is the end for which man is born."

In this carefully balanced passage Dante conveys his idea of a symmetrical social structure, culminating in a super-state, which by ensuring unbroken peace shall foster the development of all its subordinate parts and protect the individual in his pursuit of happiness. It is a dream, doubtless unrealizable. Only in the Church of Rome does such a perfect

organization exist on earth. In Dante's Heaven we
find a corresponding social structure, with grade
after grade, and with God at its apex. Even in his
Hell we see the same structural symmetry, but inverted, with Satan not at its highest but at its
lowest extremity. From one point of view, Heaven
counterbalances Hell; from another point of view, it
is Heaven and Earth that are in counterpoise, and
similarly Church balances State. It is the disturb-
ance of the balance, the breaking of the symmetry,
that causes most of the general ills of mankind.

> Two suns had Rome, when Romans walked aright;
>   Two paths they showed, — the pathway of the Lord,
>   The pathway of the world, — with double light.
> Now one hath quencht the other; and the sword
>   Hath joined the crozier. Wrong it is that one
>   Compel the other to enforced accord.
>   [*Purg.*, xvi, 106–111.]

"Two ends hath yon indescribable Providence
therefore set for man to pursue," declares our author in his *Monarchy* (iii, xvi), "to wit, the happiness of this life, which consists in the exercise of his
own virtue, and is symbolized by the Earthly Paradise; and the happiness of life eternal, which consists in the enjoyment of the divine presence, to
which man's own virtue cannot rise unless it be
aided by divine light, and which is understood as
the Heavenly Paradise. And to these happinesses,
as to different goals, man must come by different
means."

Balance, symmetry, which determine the structure of the world of spirit and the world of matter, which underlie the ideal social and political organization of mankind, which are perfectly exemplified in all the works of God, must be attempted and should be approximated in the conduct and in the products of man.

Among human products, that one which most readily lends itself to harmonic development is art; for art has in it something of the divine creative principle, and art is less than other human activities influenced by selfish interest. In music, in poetry, in painting, sculpture, and architecture is the closest worldly approach to the symmetry of things divine. And in the whole reach of human art the works most divinely symmetrical in their ordered multiplicity are the Gothic cathedral and the *Divine Comedy* of Dante.

At the close of his *Purgatory*, our poet, who has just tasted the sweet, purifying, quickening waters of the Garden of Eden, declares that he gladly would linger to impart to his readers some inkling of that draught, did not the plan of his poem forbid.

> Had I, O reader, further pages free,
>   I fain would sing (though were it but to start)
>   That sweetest draught, which ne'er had sated me.
> But since for this, my poem's second part,
>   The sheets predestined all are written full,
>   My song is halted by the check of art.
>   [*Purg.*, XXXIII, 136–141.]

A most significant phrase is this: "the check of art." For art is by no means an unchecked outpour of expression: it is a union of conception and selection, a union in which neither mate must subdue the other. As the proper balance of character is attained only by developing some tendencies and curbing others, so the artistic masterpiece is achieved only by the coupling of creative energy with restraint. If either partner predominate unduly, the result is a school of art, or a whole epoch of civilization, bereft of the equilibrium of real beauty — an art which is too indiscriminately exuberant or too barrenly severe, a period whose climate is too hot or too cold. If the eighteenth century seems to many an age of artistic frigidity, it is certain that to-day we are traversing an interglacial epoch of over-rank growth, and have especial need to mark Dante's words, "the check of art," to ponder over them, and to observe how the master illustrates his principle in his works.

Consider for a moment Dante's early book, that autobiography written before he was thirty, the *New Life*. An "autobiography" it is rightly called; but for discreetness, elusiveness, reticence, it is the strangest autobiography ever penned: an autobiography whose author never names himself, or his native city, or his best friend, or his sister, or the other friends and acquaintances who flit ghostlike through his pages — or, in fact, anyone save two ladies whose names are so marvelously appropriate that, as evidence of divine intent, they must not be suppressed. Yet, despite such reserve, what autobiography has ever surpassed it in charm, in persistence of appeal? Of the material events of the author's life we learn nothing, or next to nothing; he never mentions his parents, his station in life, his habitual occupations; we are not told who he is or what he is about. These are not the matters selected as the theme of the "little book": it is not the story of a man's life, but the story of one phase of a human soul; and the "check of art" excludes all that bears not on the subject.

In its arrangement the *New Life* is as harmoniously structural as it is consistently selective in its material. This trait is the more astonishing in that the work represents, not a single effort, but a literary activity extending over some ten years. From the poems composed since he was seventeen years old, the author and editor, then a man of twenty-eight or so, selected those which best illustrated his theme, and, arranging them in chronological sequence, embedded them in a prose narrative that expounded their true significance in the light of later events and later knowledge. The story falls — though no such division is marked in the text — into three parts almost precisely equal in length: first the author's inner life under the influence of Beatrice, before his conversion to Platonic love and the "sweet new style"; second, his Platonic devotion until her

death; third, her influence after her passing. The
conversion to serenity is preceded by a short series
of three poems teeming with a spirit of restless, unbalanced desire; preceding the thunderbolt of death,
on the other hand, is a little series of three poems of
heavenly calm and gladness. A startling premoni-
tion of impending disaster comes, as a feverish
dream, in the exact middle of the narrative; the
vision of the Lady's soul in Paradise falls at the
end, balancing the first sight of her earthly form, at
the beginning. Two early poems on the death of
a friend of Beatrice balance two late ones on the
death of a friend of her brother. Dante's homage to
the two "screen" ladies finds its counterpart in his
devotion to the gentle lady at the window. Three
magnificent odes, in the middle part of the work,
constitute, so to speak, its chief structural supports:
of these, the first, in bold hyperbole, declares that
Beatrice is too good for this earth, that Heaven is
incomplete without her; the second relates an agon-
ized, delirious dream of her death; the third pictures
her restoration to her heavenly home, and the desolation of the bereaved earth. In addition to these
three central poems, there are twenty-eight lesser
pieces of verse, to wit, twenty-five sonnets, one
ballad, one half-ode, one detached stanza; and these
twenty-eight are so grouped about the great three
as to form a distinct though concealed pattern,
wherein the minor and the major poems are thus re-

lated: ten minor, one major, four minor, one major, four minor, one major, ten minor; or ten, *one*, four, *one*, four, *one*, ten.

The oftener one peruses, the more one discovers of carefully arranged balances in this seemingly ingenuous and spontaneous work. And these balances, unperceived as they are by the casual reader, nevertheless contribute to his total impression; even as a man quite ignorant of music may be deeply stirred by a scientific arrangement of tones, so a reader may be strangely moved by the *New Life*, without consciousness of its harmonies. The reaction is strongest, as it should be, at the close, where the composition converges to its climax. Few conclusions are as satisfying as that final sonnet in which the poet tells how his thought, soaring upward like a sigh from his heart, pierces all the nine revolving heavens, even the outermost and greatest, until it reaches the true Paradise and there beholds Lady Beatrice resplendent among the blest.

Beyond the sphere that all-encircling sways,
   A sigh, escaping from my heart, doth fare.
   An insight new, which Love, so full of care,
Inspireth now, impels it up always.
When it has reacht the goal for which it prays,
   It sees a lady, full of glory there,
   And on her light, which shines beyond compare,
The pilgrim spirit wondering doth gaze.
'Tis all so strange that when it tells me this,
   I cannot comprehend, it puzzles so
     The mournful heart which ever bids it tell.

> It speaketh of that gentle one, I know,
> Because it often nameth Beatrice;
> And that, dear ladies mine, I hear full well.
>> [*Vita Nuova*, Sonnet xxv:
>> translation from *The Power of Dante*, 155.]

Now the sonnet that goes before, separated from this last one by a page or two of prose, seems at first inspection to have no connection with it; and the critic wonders why it, rather than one of the other poems, was put in this place, and why this place, rather than another, was assigned to it. The sonnet in question — an undeniably pretty one — is addressed to a company of pilgrims who from afar are traversing Florence, on their way to view the Image of the Saviour in Rome.

> Ah! pilgrims, who so thoughtful walk and slow,
> Intent perhaps on nothing near at hand,
> Come ye indeed from such a distant strand
> As your impassive faces seem to show,
> Which are not wet with tears, the while ye go
> Right through the saddest city of the land
> Like foreign men, who seem to understand
> Nothing whatever of the city's woe?
> In sooth my sighing heart is sure of this:
> That if, to hear, your journey ye defer,
>   Ye shall not then depart without a tear.
> Our mourning town hath lost its Beatrice!
> And every word which men may speak of her
>   Hath power to turn to sorrow those who hear.
>> [*Vita Nuova*, Sonnet xxiv:
>> translation from *The Ladies of Dante's Lyrics*, 123–124.]

Now the idea common to these two sonnets is the idea of pilgrimage; and in his explanatory prose

Dante is careful to observe that the word "pilgrim" is most properly applied to one who seeks the goal of his sacred desire far, very far from his native land. The two poems offer a picture of earthly and of heavenly pilgrimage. In the one, human pilgrims, in quest of a sight of the Lord's countenance, travel through the sad world that has lost its Bestower of Blessings. In the other, Dante's spirit, on a long pilgrimage to Paradise, finds there its beloved, enthroned and glorious in the world to which she belongs.

The theme of this final sonnet of the *New Life*, a pilgrimage to the other world, expands into the matter of the whole *Divine Comedy*. So inclusive is this great work that one does not at first appreciate the full range of the author's process of selection. Like the earlier book, the *Comedy* is the biography of a soul; but here the protagonist does not conceal his identity. He names his city and country, a few of his remote ancestors, distant relatives, and friends, the season of his birth, even himself. He refers in passing to several events of his material career, such as his presence at the siege of Caprona and a puzzling incident in which he figured in the Baptistery of Florence, and he presents a brief but infinitely touching picture of his exile. Never, here or elsewhere, does he name his parents, his wife or his children: these are figures unnecessary to his purpose and too intimate for irrelevant introduction. It is when we think of them, and of all the rich material offered by his various activities, that we begin to estimate Dante's exercise of the principle of exclusion.

Let us consider the subject from another point of view. The *Comedy* is in essence a vision of life after death. There are many such visions, and they are usually portrayed as such, with an introduction telling of the dreamer's previous doings and the circumstances of his dream, and an epilogue narrating his awakening and subsequent experience. Dante has none of this. Abruptly he begins with the consciousness of being lost in a dark wood and struggling to escape; abruptly he closes with the merging of his will in the cosmic will of his Maker. Nowhere does he call his journey a vision or a dream. The superfluous framework of the conventional visionary type is all discarded; discarded, too, is all needless identification of the supernaturally journeying soul with the bodily Dante who walked the streets of Florence.

Nevertheless, the poem is a personal confession; to seal that confession he once, and only once, declares his name. It is a confession of sin, of remorse, of ethical reflection, of reformation and discipline and purification, of spiritual uplifting into perfect accord with God. All this is set forth in the allegorical form of a journey through Hell, Purgatory, and Heaven. Allegorically the dark wood is the poet's own state of moral blindness; the ugly pains of Hell picture the sinful world from which he revolts and labors to emerge; the mountain of Purgatory is a symbol of spiritual cleansing; the Garden of Eden represents innocence regained; the ascent from heaven to heaven into the very presence of the Lord portrays the stages of mystic contemplation whose goal is fulfilment of the divine promise: "Blessed are the pure in heart, for they shall see God."

Once more, then, we find a wondrous symmetry, a correspondence between the universe, from the depths of Hell to the heights of the Empyrean, and the successive experiences of the soul rising from sin to beatitude. Step by step the parallelism is manifest. Each punishment in Hell matches a sin, each heaven above is equated with a stage of spiritual advancement. The vastest of all themes, the theme of human sin and salvation, is adjusted to the great plan of the universe.

Symmetrically balanced in its conception, the *Divine Comedy* is equally symmetrical in its outer form. Three, the mystic number of the Holy Trinity, is the number of its books; thirty-three, the number of cantos in each book. One introductory canto raises the total to a hundred, the square of the "perfect number," ten. The whole poem is written in interlocking groups of three lines. The three books correspond to the three realms of the departed. Each leads up in climax to a culminating figure — the figure of Satan, of Beatrice, of God. Three blessed ladies watch over Dante in his hour of peril; three guides direct him, Virgil, Beatrice, St. Bernard. Virgil, or Reason, shows him the true nature of sin and the means of surmounting it; Beatrice, or Revelation, conducts him up the grades of religious contemplation; Bernard, or Intuition, prepares him to see God.

Thus is Dante led from the unbalanced state of sin to the poise of complete conformity to the divine plan. No longer is he unlike "the centre of a circle, to which the parts of the circumference bear the same relation"; for "as a wheel in even revolution," his will is turned "by that Love which moves the sun and the other stars."

Chapter VI

"ALL MEN NATURALLY DESIRE TO KNOW"

THE feast of knowledge which Dante prepared for the world, under the title of the *Banquet*, opens thus: "As the Philosopher saith at the beginning of the *First Philosophy*, 'All men naturally desire to know'; the reason whereof may be that everything, stamped by Providence with a nature of its own, is inclined to perfect itself; wherefore, inasmuch as knowledge is the ultimate perfection of our soul, in which our ultimate happiness consists, we are all naturally subject to a craving for it. Nevertheless, many are deprived of this noblest perfection by different causes which, either within a man or outside him, remove him from the habit of knowledge."

Two internal and two external obstacles to knowledge Dante specifies. The inner impediments are bodily infirmity and vicious tastes, especially idleness; the outer ones are family and civic affairs and lack of opportunity. In each pair, the first member, according to our author, is an unavoidable hindrance and therefore a valid excuse for ignorance: bodily imperfection, domestic and public business — these and these alone — are invincible obstacles. The other impediments can be overcome: opportunity can be made, difficult though the task may be; vicious habits can and should be conquered. As excuses, these drawbacks, especially the second, are worthy, not of indulgence, but of "blame and abomination."

Such is Dante's severe judgment on those who, for any reason short of absolute necessity, follow not the natural human impulse of self-perfection by knowledge. "O blessed those few who sit at the table where is eaten the bread of the angels, and wretched they who share the food of cattle!" The "bread of the angels," of course, is truth. Only in the attainment of truth can man find happiness, since "the ultimate perfection of our soul is knowledge." Without that angelic food, we must ever be as the souls in Dante's Limbus, plagued with a longing eternally unfulfilled, hungering for something they need but possess not — those gently plaintive souls that dwell in everlasting darkness and set the air a-quiver with their sighs. They had never drunk the draught of truth for which the woman of Samaria once asked.

"Jesus answered and said unto her, Whosoever drinketh of this water shall thirst again: But whosoever drinketh of the water that I shall give him shall never thirst. . . . The woman saith unto him, Sir, give me this water, that I thirst not." — John iv, 13-15.

No one more than Dante ever thirsted for that water, and no one strove more ardently to quench that thirst.

> That inborn thirst, which nothing else can slake
>> Than water such as that whose gracious draught
>> The woman of Samaria fain would take
> Tormented me.

> La sete natural, che mai non sazia
>> Se non con l' acqua onde la femminetta
>> Sammaritana domandò la grazia,
> Mi tormentava.   [*Purg.*, XXI, 1-4.]

What is the truth? The old question arises again. What did Dante mean by knowledge? What was the water for which he thirsted? Knowledge, for him, included much: it comprehended not only physical science and philosophy, but also divinely revealed truth; and it embraced even intuition, which transcends science and understanding. Dante would be satisfied with nothing short of the whole scale of knowledge, from observation to immediate perception. It will be profitable to follow him in his quest, to observe the problems that most interested him, the questions that he found hardest.

"Two goals, then, hath yon indescribable Providence set for the pursuit of man," declares Dante in his *Monarchy*, III, xvi: "to wit, the happiness of this life, which consists in the exercise of our own virtue, and is represented by the Earthly Paradise; and the happiness of life eternal, which consists in the enjoyment of the divine presence, whereto our own virtue cannot attain, unless it be helped by divine light, and which is signified by the Heavenly Paradise. And to these happinesses, as to different ends, we must come by different means." To the first we come, he avers, by means of philosophical teachings, making use of the moral and intellectual virtues; to the second, by means of spiritual teachings which surpass human reason, making use of the theological virtues. Our leaders to the first are the philosophers; our guide to the second is revelation. Thus, in the *Divine Comedy*, Virgil, or human reason, leads the poet to the Earthly Paradise, whereas he reaches the Heavenly Paradise only under the direction of Beatrice, or revelation.

What constitutes the happiness of this life, the happiness symbolized as the Garden of Eden? From Dante's utterances we may infer that in his opinion its ingredients are these: cleanness, activity, fame, widsom, knowledge. Of innocence the lovely and undying type in the great poem is Matilda, the maiden genius of the Terrestrial Paradise. Without purity, there can be no unalloyed gladness. Matilda is almost the image of Leah (whom Dante recalls in a dream), traditionally the type of innocent activity. As representatives of the busy life we may take Trajan, the just ruler; Cacciaguida, the crusader, the poet's ancestor; Justinian, the lawgiver; also St. Francis and St. Dominic, the preachers and founders, whom, be it noted, our author regards not primarily as contemplative but as active spirits. Constant useful doing is an important factor in mundane happiness. Another is fame, the result of active service. Fame was very dear to Dante; he craved both literary and social distinction, proud of his art and of his ancestry. Political and moral leadership he desired as well, but, it would seem, rather for the benefit of others than for his own gratification. Artistic fame is represented in the *Comedy* by the poets Guido Guinizelli and Arnaut Daniel, by Virgil and his companions in the Noble Castle, by Oderisi, the miniaturist of Gubbio; the fame of militant religion, by St. Dominic and by Folquet de Marselha, the troubadour bishop, whose soul in Paradise is pointed out to Dante, with these words: "Of this bright and precious jewel of our heaven, which is closest to me, great fame has remained, and ere it die, this centennial year shall yet be fived. See whether man should attain excellence, that the first life may leave another life behind!"

> "Di questa luculenta e cara gioia
> Del nostro cielo, che più m' è propinqua,
> Grande fama rimase, e pria che moia
> Questo centesim' anno ancor s'incinqua.
> Vedi se far si dee l' uomo eccellente,
> Sì ch' altra vita la prima relinqua!"
>
> [*Par.*, IX, 37–42.]

Dante's own eager desire is betrayed by his question whether, in order not to lose every chance of

refuge in his exile, he shall withhold some part of the
things disclosed to him concerning the iniquity of
the great, or shall boldly tell the worst, sacrificing
safety to fame: "If I am a timid friend to truth, I
fear to lose life among those who shall call this time
ancient."

> E s' io al vero son timido amico,
>   Temo di perder viver tra coloro
>   Che questo tempo chiameranno antico.
>   [*Par.*, xvii, 118–120.]

The response is the decision we should have expected: fearlessly to proclaim everything, regardless
of material consequences.

A confession of Dante's cherished ambition is
found, near the close of the *Paradise*, in those verses
already quoted:

> If fate ordain my sacred poem here,
>   Which heaven and earth so amply have supplied
>   That it hath kept me lean this many a year,
> Shall melt the hate that locketh me outside
>   My pretty fold, where once I slept a lamb
>   Whom hostile wolves with their devices tried,
> With louder voice and fleet of stalwart ram
>   Returning, on mine own baptismal font
>   Shall I be crowned a poet, as I am.
>   [*Par.*, xxv, 1–9.]

A pathetic hope, for it was destined never to be
realized. In the course of his poetic vision, however,
he does find recognition, and from the highest authorities, the shades of the great departed singers.
Virgil, Homer, Ovid, Lucan, Horace receive him in

their company, and he is "sixth amid all this wisdom." When first he beholds their majestic forms, he questions Virgil: "O thou who honorest both science and art, who are these, who have such honor that it distinguishes them from the fashion of the others?" And Virgil replies: "Their honored renown, which reëchoes in thy life, wins grace in Heaven which grants them such precedence."

> "O tu che onori e scienza ed arte,
>   Questi chi son, ch' hanno cotanta onranza
>   Che dal modo degli altri li diparte?"
> E quegli a me: "L' onrata nominanza
>   Che di lor suona su nella tua vita
>   Grazia acquista nel ciel che sì gli avanza."
>   [*Inf.*, IV, 73–78.]

For the highest earthly bliss, as for "honored renown," wisdom and knowledge are needful. Knowledge is not wisdom: the former is acquired, the latter is inborn. From the stars that shape our disposition we derive receptivity, the power to acquire. Insight is bestowed by grace accorded us when, at birth, our souls are created; it may come later, as a special revelation, to a soul in a state of charity. The harvest garnered from our gifts depends upon our use of our own free will. The wisest among all men was Christ. Of purely human beings, the wisest was Adam, who was fashioned directly by God. Wisdom does not grow. Knowledge grows, being the fruit of intellectual curiosity, which increases by what it feeds on. Intellectual curiosity, that "concreated

and perpetual thirst" which endlessly tormented
our poet, showing him, beyond every peak he
climbed, a further and higher one, made ignorance
a plague well-nigh unbearable.

> No ignorance ever made me crave to know
>   And put my wits to such a sorry rout
>   (Unless my memory errs, which tells me so)
> As then I seemed to suffer in my doubt.
>   To ask, our hurried course I dared not stay;
>   And nothing by myself could I find out.
> Thus timid, thoughtful, I pursued my way.

> Nulla ignoranza mai con tanta guerra
>   Mi fe' desideroso di sapere,
>   Se la memoria mia in ciò non erra,
> Quanta pare'mi allor pensando avere;
>   Nè per la fretta domandarn' er' oso,
>   Nè per me lì potea cosa vedere.
> Così m' andava timido e pensoso.
>   [*Purg.*, xx, 145–151.]

Proportionate to the agony of thirst is the rapture
of satisfaction — at least, until the insatiable desire
to know shall parch the lips again, led by a fresh
mirage. The very expectation of an immediate
answer floods the questioner with comfort. So it
befalls our dreamer, when Virgil puts the very question which Dante had longed, but had not dared, to
ask.

> This query threaded so the needle's eye
>   Of my desire that with the hope alone
>   My withering thirst forthwith was not so dry.

Sì mi die' domandando per la cruna
  Del mio disio che pur con la speranza
  Si fece la mia sete men digiuna.

[*Purg.*, xxi, 37–39.]

This thirst for knowledge it is, this "mind ever eager for new things," that made Dante so sympathetic with Ulysses, the great explorer. Ulysses was a wicked man, a deceiver, and therefore merits Hell, where the poet finds him; but he was a tireless seeker for knowledge, therefore a brother, and, to the inquiring soul, the most romantic of all sailors over "perilous seas in faery lands forlorn." Even his eternal punishment in the lower world is romantic. A dark valley is spangled with walking flames, which from above look like fireflies in the dusk; within each flame is the soul of one who misused the divine gift of eloquence. When the spirit talks, the vibration of its speech is little by little imparted to the enveloping flame, which, waving to and fro like a tongue, utters aloud the words formed by the soul within it. One flame, unlike the others, has two peaks; for inside it are two spirits, Ulysses and Diomed, inseparable in death as in life. At Dante's prayer, Virgil inquires of the taller tip, wherein Ulysses is hidden, how and where the great traveler met his end.

The higher horn that capt the ancient pyre
  Forthwith began to murmur and to dip,
  And flickered like a wind-tormented fire;
Then waving to and fro its topmost tip,
  The likeness of a talking tongue it wore,
  And utterance articulate let slip.

"When I left Circe, who a year and more
  Delayed me near Gaëta by the sea
  (Before Æneas ever named that shore),
No tenderness for child, nor sympathy
  For aged sire, nor love legitimate
  Which should have gladdened my Penelope,
Had power my inborn passion to abate
  To know the world, its every nook and crook,
  The good and evil of our human state.
O'er open deep once more my course I took;
  A single ship had I, a tiny band
  Of comrades who my side had ne'er forsook.
I visited the shore on either hand,
  Morocco, Spain, Sardinia did I spy;
  And, in that sea, each wave-encompast land.
Full stiff and old my fellows were, and I,
  When finally we reacht the narrow cleft
  Where Hercules his pillars lifted high,
A mark for man, of further flight bereft.
  Sebilia then I past upon my right;
  Already Septa faded on the left.
'Brethren,' I spake, 'thro' many and many a plight,
  Despising dangers, ye have reacht the West.
  Few moments now remain before the night
Enfold your senses in eternal rest.
  Permit this fleeting eventide to scan
  Th' unpeopled world, in sun-pursuing quest.
Consider what a noble thing is man!
  Ye were not born to ruminate like kine,
  But to achieve what wit and valor can.'
My comrades I so keenly did incline,
  With this harangue, untraveled ways to learn,
  That scarce had they been checkt by words of mine.
And, leaving all the morning skies astern,
  With flapping oars we winged our reckless flight;
  But ever to the left our course did turn.

Already all the stars were seen by night
  Of th' other pole, and ours so downward bent,
  The sea's horizon hid it from our sight.
Five times rekindled, and as many spent,
  Beneath the moon was all its monthly sheen,
  While we upon our mighty journey went.
Then hove in sight a mount, of misty mien,
  So far away it was; and towered so
  That I its mate for height had never seen.
Great joy was ours, but soon it turned to woe:
  On that new shore a whirlwind did begin,
  And swept upon our bow with sudden blow.
Three times it made the boat and waters spin,
  And, at the fourth, lifted our stern amain;
  At Someone's beck, our stem went plunging in,
Till over us the ocean closed again."

             [*Inf.*, xxvi, 85–142:
           translation from *Dante*, 214–216.]

Such was Dante's idea of worldly bliss: incessant
quest of knowledge, making the most of every talent
the stars have bestowed, and of the God-given treasure of wisdom; at the same time, ceaseless busy
service in behalf of our kind; fame, undying renown,
the result of both kinds of endeavor; cleanness of
thought and deed, "that the river of memory may
flow down through consciousness undefiled." The
active life is this, the normal life of the normal righteous man, though inferior, in principle, to the life of
contemplation, which to the pure, loving, devout
soul affords a foretaste of the transcendent joys of
Heaven.

Now what, in Dante's judgment, constituted
heavenly happiness? Understanding and intuition

we should at once infer, from what we have already seen, to be chief factors; to these we must add, if we read Dante's *Paradise* aright, fellowship and submission.

It is the pervasive atmosphere of fellowship, of brotherhood in blessedness, that gives a human charm to our poet's Paradise. Whether it be the constellated warrior-souls in Mars, who interrupt their song in order to allow the stranger opportunity to ask a question, or the lights of theology who in the sun stop their round and their music to gratify the newcomer, rejoicing to pass from one interest to another, —

> Felicitando sè di cura in cura, —
> [*Par.*, xiii, 30.]

all illustrate the doctrine that the greater the number of sharers in celestial goods, the greater the share of each partaker; for the goods of Heaven, unlike the goods of earth, are possessed by all together, and every soul that reaches Paradise receives the heavenly good, which is love, not only from God directly, but also reflected from all its fellows. The love of every blessed human creature is bestowed first of all upon God, its alpha and omega, the source of all goodness; next, as we have already learned, upon the rest of the universe in proportion to the degree of grace which God has extended to each member — that is, in proportion to each member's likeness to its Maker. Every soul, then, which has attained Heaven, is an object of love to all the others; its happiness is not complete without their affectionate partnership.

In the middle of the mystic rose of the Empyrean, St. Bernard arouses Dante from his rapt contemplation of the golden sea of grace that environs him, bidding the stranger look up and view the congregation of the blest, which rises, tier on tier, "in more than a thousand steps."

> "O son of grace, thou canst not wholly know
>   This gladsome life," the elder said to me,
>   "By gazing all-intently here below.
> The circles, e'en the furthest, shalt thou see.
>   Look upward, till thou see enthroned the Queen
>   To whom this realm does homage lovingly."
>   [*Par.*, xxxi, 112–117.]

Dante gazes aloft and round about, as he has been admonished, viewing the whole congregation of the blest.

> Faces I saw that charm to charity,
>   Lovely with inborn smiles and mirror'd light —
>   Their looks majestic all, and grand to see.
>
> Vedea di carità visi suadi,
>   D' altrui lume fregiati e del suo riso,
>   Ed atti ornati di tutte onestadi.
>   [*Par.*, xxxi, 49–51.]

An admonition not dissimilar is given earlier by Beatrice, the heavenly guide and symbol of Revelation.

"Why art thou so enraptured with my face,
    Thou turnest not to see the garden fair
    That flowers beneath the rays of Jesus' grace?"
                        [*Par.*, xxiii, 70–72.]

Once before, the sweet Bestower of Blessings has directed the poet's attention from her own eyes to her heavenly compatriots.

She vanquisht me, her smile so brightly shone,
    The while she spake, "Now turn and hark," she said,
    "For Heaven is not within my eyes alone."

Vincendo me col lume d' un sorriso,
    Ella mi disse: "Volgiti ed ascolta,
    Che non pur ne' miei occhi è Paradiso."
                        [*Par.*, xviii, 19–21.]

Of all heavenly joys, the greatest, the most peaceful, the most satisfying is the sense of perfect accord with the Creator, the merging of the individual will, without loss of individual consciousness or volition, in the will of the universe; the sacrifice of self to the universal Father. This voluntary and perpetual submission is the return that grateful souls make to the Cause of their happiness and their being. Keen as is the craving for knowledge and for vision, each soul is content with that degree of enlightenment which suits its particular capacity; for every soul is created with a grade of spiritual insight, a grade of receptivity, a grade of potential happiness and wisdom, different from those of every other soul. Each soul in Heaven knows that it receives all the blessed-

ness it can contain, and is satisfied with that, never
coveting the beatitude of a soul more highly endowed, much less the complete vision that belongs
to God alone. Why one spirit should be more richly
gifted than another, we can never know; but we are
sure that such differentiation has its good purpose
in the eternal plan, and we gladly acquiesce in the
divine ordinance. Such is the significance of the
words spoken by the great heavenly Eagle, made up
of the congregation of the souls of the just, which
addresses Dante in the sphere of Jupiter: "O predestination, how far distant is thy root from those
eyes which see not the first cause in its wholeness!
Keep a close rein, ye mortals, on your judgments;
for we, who see God, do not yet know all the elect;
and sweet to us is such a want, for our blessedness is
purified in this blessing: that what God wills, we
will."

> "Ed enne dolce così fatto scemo,
>   Perchè il ben nostro in questo ben s' affina,
>   Che quel che vuole Iddio e noi volemo."
>   [*Par.*, xx, 136–138.]

The *Divine Comedy* concludes its story with the
moment of perfect submission, the absorption of the
poet's will in the great will that governs the world.

> The strength of soaring fancy here gave way.
>   But, like a wheel whose movement nothing mars,
>   My wish and will were turned, in even sway,
> By Love, which turns the sun and all the stars.
>   [*Par.*, xxxiii, 142–145.]

Now, renunciation of the individual self is the result of seeing God, no longer "through a glass, darkly, but face to face." This is intuition, or direct apprehension, something higher than understanding, which in turn is higher than observation. When once we see God face to face, we can nevermore avert our mind or our will from him. All that we perceive, we perceive in him; all that we love, we love because of him. The vision of God, according to St. Thomas, is the "essential" or perpetual reward of the blest, the "accidental" or variable reward being the good done by themselves or by others. Intuition, the "essential reward," comes like a flash, blinding the recipient to all else.

> So high my pinions nevermore could ride,
>   Save that a lightning flash my spirit struck,
>   A flash wherein its wish was satisfied.

> Ma non eran da ciò le proprie penne,
>   Se non che la mia mente fu percossa
>   Da un fulgore in che sua voglia venne.
>   [*Par.*, xxxiii, 139–141.]

On a lower grade than this union with God, but included in its effects, is comprehension, the understanding of cause and result, the solution of baffling problems. To an intensely eager hunter for knowledge, like Dante, the prospect of an answer to his tormenting questions constitutes one of the great allurements of Paradise. Puzzles without end are challenging him, curiosity devours him; deep religious truths he accepts on faith, but cannot explain. When he shall be dead, peace will come with understanding. Things that now seem impossible to grasp will be as self-evident as axioms.

> Those things which faith commands us to receive
> We then shall see, not proven — self-revealed,
> Like any primal truth that we believe.

> Lì si vedrà ciò che tenem per fede,
> Non dimostrato, ma fia per sè noto,
> A guisa del ver primo che l' uom crede.
>
> [*Par.*, II, 43–45.]

What were the great problems that troubled Dante, the great questions to which he either sought an answer on earth or expected one in Heaven? They are of every order, physical, philological, ethical, philosophical or theological.

A physical problem with which he struggled for many years is the mystery of the spots on the moon: what makes them? When he wrote his *Banquet*, he was apparently content with the explanation that the differences in brightness are due to differences in density. But in his *Paradise* days this formula no longer satisfied him. The theory applied to the moon must also fit the stars, one of which "differeth from another in glory." Now the diverse brightness of the stars cannot be due merely to diverse degrees of density; else the stars would be all of one kind, and consequently would exert only one influence, whereas we know that the influences of the stars are manifold. On the basis of differences in kind among celestial bodies, with varying ways of receiving the divine energy and combining with it, Dante erects a whole doctrine of the relation of spirit to matter, of the transmission and differentiation of the single power that emanates from God.

Philology engaged Dante's faculties of observation and of speculation. How did speech originate? What was the first language spoken by man? Once more we find a discrepancy between the *Banquet* and the *Paradise:* further study or further reflection had caused the student to change his mind. In the earlier work, Hebrew is the primitive language, and the first word uttered by human lips is the Hebrew name of God. According to Dante's later view, whose expression he puts into the mouth of no less an authority than Adam, the first mode of speech had died away before the confusion of tongues; for language is a human product, and the products of man ceaselessly change from generation to generation.

In ethics, Dante was deeply concerned with the sanctity of vows. Indeed, so earnestly and so lengthily does he treat this topic, in his *Paradise*, that one cannot help suspecting a personal reason for his interest. A daughter of his was a nun. He was himself reported to have contemplated entering the Franciscan order. Can it be that his minute, emphatic discussion reflects a long inner struggle? If not, why does he allow it to obstruct so long our ascent to the Empyrean? The gist of his argument is that a vow, which is in the nature of a pact with God, consists of two elements: namely, the abdication of the will involved in the act of vowing; and, second, the thing that is promised. The former can never be canceled save by observance. The latter, the thing promised, may sometimes be exchanged for something harder or more precious, but only with the proper ecclesiastical sanction. The upshot is a warning against taking vows lightly.

The theological and metaphysical field is full of problems; but only three, and these three closely related, seem to have greatly troubled Dante: the problem of divine justice, of imperfection in the world, of predestination. To these he returns time and again, bravely grappling with difficulties and contradictions. The doctrine of the two natures in Christ, the doctrine of the three Persons in one Godhead, the doctrine of the Holy Ghost proceeding equally and eternally from Father and Son — these he frankly and lovingly accepted as mysterious truths incomprehensible to mortal mind here below, though clear to the spirits in Heaven; and he was content to postpone his understanding until the future life.

But justice is a present and knotty problem, although capable of solution, if approached with humility and intelligence. It was not the dogma of original sin and redemption that appeared difficult to Dante. In that, all is plain. Adam, wisest and most favored of men, contained in himself all the potentialities of mankind, and therefore in his sin involved all the issue of his flesh. To comprehend the method of redemption, we must remember that "all the paths of the Lord are mercy and truth" (Psalm xxv, 10), and that in this passage "truth" means justice. To rescue man, the Lord had open before him the path of mercy and the path of justice; save that strict justice alone would never have granted release, because no atonement within the power of humanity could have counterbalanced the presumption of Adam's disobedience. God might, then, have taken the path of mercy; but, to make his gift representative of his whole self, he chose to follow both paths, assuming man's guilt and atoning for it (*Par.*, vii, 97–120). In this matter, the accepted teaching was to our poet both beautiful and clear.

No: in the field of justice, it was quite a different question that vexed Dante. We know that it did vex him, because he argues it so elaborately, and because he prefaces and interlards his argument with such solemn warnings against presumption. Justice, he assures us, is naught else than God's will; to say that God is unjust is, therefore, a contradiction of terms, as we have already had occasion to observe. Indeed, if we were not really convinced that the Lord is always just, we should not be so shocked at

an apparent injustice; our very horror is proof of
our confidence.

> When heavenly justice seems to us unjust,
>   That mortal seeming is a proof of faith,
>   Not of perverse, heretical mistrust.

> Parere ingiusta la nostra giustizia
>   Negli occhi dei mortali è argomento
>   Di fede, e non d' eretica nequizia.
> [Par., IV, 67–69.]

It is only our restricted, clouded vision that con-
ceals from us the true purpose underlying the sundry happenings whereof we are cognizant. It is not
for us, "with sight no longer than a span, to judge
of things a thousand miles away." Even when the
eternal purpose seems to change, to be influenced by
entreaty, — as in the case of St. Gregory, who by his
intercession obtained salvation for the pagan emperor Trajan, or of Hezekiah, whose prayer was
answered by a prolongation of his life for fifteen
years, — we must be assured that both prayer and
response are but a part of the universal plan, fore-
seen by God from all eternity. The very merit of
Gregory, or of Hezekiah, is a result of divine grace.

> O earthly creatures, minds of babyhood!
>   The primal Will, intrinsically right,
>   Hath ne'er revoked itself, the highest good.
> That word is just which doth that Will recite.
>   No secondary goodness bends that Will:
>   The Will begets the goodness with its light.

O terreni animali, o menti grosse!
  La prima Volontà, ch' è per sè buona,
  Da sè, ch' è Sommo Ben, mai non si mosse.
Cotanto è giusto quanto a lei consuona.
  Nullo creato bene a sè la tira,
  Ma essa radiando lui cagiona.

[*Par.*, xix, 85–90.]

Now, the particular question with which Dante
wrestled is the justice of the fate of virtuous pagans,
those righteous men of old who knew not Christ and
therefore cannot attain salvation. Virgil himself,
the poet's guide, is one of these. As the ancient
Mantuan approaches his companions, after a brief
visit to the world above, he turns pallid with pity —
so pale, indeed, that Dante thinks he is afraid, until
he explains: "The anguish of the people here below
paints on my face the compassion that thou takest
for fear." "Thou askest not," he continues, "what
are these spirits which thou seest. Now I will have
thee know, before going further, that they sinned
not; and if they had deserts, it is not enough, for
they had not baptism, which is a part of the faith
thou believest; and if they lived before Christianity,
they did not properly adore God. And of these am
I myself. Because of such a lack, not for any other
fault, we are lost; and we suffer only in this, that we
live in longing without hope."

Why should such souls be condemned? As the
query is phrased in the *Divine Comedy*, —

"A man is born on Indus' distant strand;
 And there is none to read or write or teach
 Of Christ, or speak of him, on any hand.
As far as ever human sight can reach,
 Upright in will, he does his duty well,
 Sinless in life and innocent in speech.
He dieth unbaptized, an infidel.
 What fault is his, if he believeth not?
 What kind of justice sendeth him to Hell?"

Chè tu dicevi: "Un uom nasce alla riva
 Dell' Indo, e quivi non è chi ragioni
 Di Cristo, nè chi legga, nè chi scriva;
E tutti i suoi voleri ed atti buoni
 Sono, quanto ragione umana vede,
 Senza peccato in vita o in sermoni.
More non battezzato e senza fede:
 Ov' è questa giustizia che il condanna?
 Ov' è la colpa sua, se ei non crede?"

[*Par.*, xix, 70–78.]

The answer, when at last we come to it, is simple.
A man in pagan time or country who leads a noble
life, without sin, is not lost. He could not thus conduct himself without God's grace; and that same
grace reveals to him the essentials of true faith,
which are hidden from others. Again and again,
says St. Thomas, has God's mysterious favor thus
illumined the heathen and led them to salvation.

The existence of evil is not so readily explained;
but it is involved in the doctrine of free will. God
created angels and men, that there might be other
beings to share his happiness. Now these beings
could not be "other," separate, conscious creatures,

unless they had freedom of choice between evil and
good. Hence the possibility of evil is implied in the
very possibility of achieving salvation. Why evil so
often seems to prevail is a mystery. In a passing
reference to Phaëthon, Dante declares that in his
case Jove was mysteriously just: his justice is manifest in the punishment of Phaëthon's audacity; but
why God allowed him to do such great harm is beyond our understanding. Justice is there, though
we see it not.

> The comprehension of humanity
>   Can penetrate eternal righteousness
>   No more than human eye can pierce the sea.
> From shore, the eye the ocean's bed may guess,
>   But on the main 't is hidden by its depth;
>   Yet there it lies, though hidden, none the less.
>
> Però nella giustizia sempiterna
>   La vista che riceve il vostro mondo,
>   Com' occhio per lo mar, dentro s' interna;
> Chè benchè dalla proda veggia il fondo,
>   In pelago nol vede; e nondimeno
>   È lì, ma cela lui l' esser profondo.
>   [*Par.*, XIX, 58–63.]

In the ultimate triumph of goodness Dante had
perfect confidence, as he solemnly testifies in his
repeated prophecies.

Of the general problem of imperfection in the universe Dante apparently found no satisfactory solution. He returns to it persistently, but his explana-
tions are baffling to the reader, if not to him. God's

universal plan is perfect; the realization, accomplished with the medium of matter, falls below the divine idea, because matter is imperfect. Yet matter, created directly by God, should be perfect, as are all things immediately fashioned by him. The imperfection seems to be due to the moulding of brute matter by secondary agents, the stars; but these, too, are the work of God's hand. We may say, if we choose, that while created material things are perfect of their kind, their perfection is of a lower order. Even thus, there seems to be a break in the chain of argument; and, in point of fact, Dante never plainly makes such an assertion. Perhaps "imperfection" is used in two senses: created things may be regarded as perfect in themselves, though necessarily imperfect in relation to their Maker.

Another apparent contradiction, irreconcilable by unaided human intelligence, is the seeming conflict between predestination and free will. But this is avowedly a mystery. Foreknowledge by an omnipotent Creator does not impair liberty of conduct on the part of the beings whom he has created. The plan is determined from eternity; our minds are shaped by the stars, directed by the Lord's angelic ministers; our souls are created, all different, by the Lord himself. Yet we remain free to choose between good and bad. Here the mystery lies, unfathomable. Says Virgil, in Dante's *Purgatory:* "Mad is he who hopes that our reason can traverse the infinite way

followed by one Substance in three Persons. Be
satisfied, O human race, to argue from the effect; for
had ye been able to see all, there had been no need
for Mary to bear child, and some whom ye have seen
fruitlessly longing would have had their craving
stilled, which is given them to their eternal sadness.
I am speaking of Aristotle and of Plato, and of many
others." And at this, Dante adds, Virgil "bowed
his head and said no more, remaining sorrowful."

> "Matto è chi spera che nostra ragione
> Possa trascorrer la infinita via
> Che tiene una sustanzia in tre persone.
> State contenti, umana gente, al *quia;*
> Chè se potuto aveste veder tutto,
> Mestier non era partorir Maria;
> E disiar vedeste senza frutto
> Tai che sarebbe lor disio quetato,
> Ch' eternalmente è dato lor per lutto.
> Io dico d' Aristotele e di Plato
> E di molti altri." E qui chinò la fronte,
> E più non disse, e rimase turbato.
>
> [*Purg.*, III, 34–45.]

Of like tenor is the answer (mentioned earlier) of
Peter Damian, the great ascetic, who comes down to
meet Dante in the Heaven of Saturn, where contemplative spirits make their appearance. When the
poet asks him why he, Peter Damian, rather than
any other monastic soul, has been predestined to
greet him in this sphere, he replies thus: "Whatsoever soul is most enlightened in Heaven, whatsoever
Seraph bends his eye most intently on God, would
not satisfy thy asking; for what thou inquirest is

sunk so far beyond, in the abyss of the eternal statute, that it is severed from every created vision."

Each individual plays, of his own volition, his
allotted part; but why that part was assigned him,
he may never know. All are created with different
endowments. No two of the well-nigh countless host
of angels are alike; no two souls are alike. Every
spirit sees God in its own way; and on its manner of
seeing God depend its love and its joy.

Yet all angels and all human souls — and they
alone — have the gift of free will, and, with it, responsibility. Other creatures, animal, vegetable,
and mineral, automatically follow their instinct, and
can do no wrong. Angels and men alone are free to
do wrong, and, consequently, by doing right, are
capable of achieving Paradise. "The greatest gift,"
says Beatrice, "that God in creation gave in his
bounty, the gift most in conformity with his goodness, the gift he prizes highest, was freedom of the
will, wherewith intelligent creatures, all of them, and
they alone, were and are endowed."

> "Lo maggior don che Dio per sua larghezza
>   Fesse creando, ed alla sua bontate
>   Più conformato, e quel ch' ei più apprezza,
> Fu della volontà la libertate,
>   Di che le creature intelligenti,
>   E tutte e sole, furo e son dotate."
>   [*Par.*, v, 19–24.]

The angels made their choice, once for all, at the
beginning. Created with grace sufficient for use of
their freedom, sufficient to see things as they are,

they were offered the full measure of grace, with
vision into divine wisdom, and therefore with complete love: some, in their pride, rejected the proffer,
fell, and became demons down below. Others accepted, and, seeing God so clearly, could never more
deviate from his will. Man has the gift open to him
throughout his mortal life. His will is adequate, if
he but follow the light given him. When mankind
goes astray, "the fault is not in the stars, but in ourselves"; else there were no justice in penalty or
recompense. Though our impulses may be beyond
our control, dependent on the stars, inherent in circumstances or in disposition, we have conscience
and free election. If we fail, the blame is all our own.

While the gain or loss of Heaven lies in the exercise of our will, the degree or sort of happiness we
enjoy on high, if saved, depends on the measure of
our vision; and that is a matter of grace, of mysterious predestination. Heaven is a vast symphony of
different kinds of beatitude, amidst the wheeling
skies.

> From different mortal voices come sweet peals.
>   Thus different seats in this our heavenly life
>   Render sweet harmony amidst the wheels.

> Diverse voci fan giù dolci note;
>   Così diversi scanni in nostra vita
>   Rendon dolce armonia tra queste rote.
>   [*Par.*, VI, 124–126.]

Yet all are content. Every soul, knowing that it
receives perfect blessedness according to its foreor-

dained capacity, gladdened by the happiness of its fellows, rejoices in its conformity to God's will. This assurance, conveyed to Dante by the nun, Piccarda, sister of his friend Forese Donati, opens the poet's eyes to the true character of heavenly bliss.

> Then it was clear to me how everywhere
>   In Heaven is Paradise; and yet the grace
>   Of joy supreme rains variously there.

> Chiaro mi fu allor com' ogni dove
>   In cielo è Paradiso, e sì la grazia
>   Del sommo ben d' un modo non vi piove.
>   [*Par.*, III, 88–90.]

All spirits are different, each has its own individuality, like a color in the rainbow; but, like the rainbow hues, all are blended in the white light of the divine will.

In these theological teachings, so beautifully instilled by the poet, we find two helpful lessons. One is the wholesome doctrine of responsibility. Whatever the force of circumstances, whatever the weaknesses of disposition, every human being has the power and the duty to achieve ultimate peace. The other is the conviction that in the predestined scheme of the universe there is a fit place for every one of God's creatures. Every one of us has his own mansion assigned him. Though despite all his endeavor he find it not on earth, he will find it among the many in his Father's house.

Chapter VII

THE CHOICE OF A THEME

Sumite materiam vestris qui scribitis aequam
Viribus; et versate diu, quid ferre recusent
Quid valeant humeri.
[Horace, *Epistola ad Pisones*, 38–40.]

"BEFORE all things," declares Dante in his treatise *On Vernacular Composition*, "before all things it behooves everyone to adapt to his own shoulders the weight of his theme, lest one be forced to stumble into the mire, because the strength of his shoulders is overladen. That is what our master Horace counsels, when he says at the beginning of his *Poetics:* 'Choose your theme.'" It is not without interest to ask what Dante had to choose from, when he started his literary career. What possibilities were suggested to him by the literature he knew? To answer this question, we must ask another: what literature did he know in the years when, having studied out for himself the art of versemaking, he began to compose songs of his own? His earliest poem, as far as we are aware, is that first sonnet of the *New Life*, written when he was seventeen and, having received a greeting from Beatrice, became conscious of love:

On every captive soul and gentle heart
  Before whose eyes the present screed may go,
  Greetings from Love, their master, I bestow,
And beg, their judgment they to me impart.
Of all the time when stars display their art
  The hours bethirded were, or nearly so,
  When Love appeared before me, nothing slow.
At thought of him I still with horror start!
Joyous to see was Love, and he did keep
  My heart within his hand, and in his arms
My Lady, lightly wrapt, in slumber deep.
Then on this burning heart, aroused from sleep,
  He poorly fed her, deaf to her alarms.
And as he went away, I saw him weep.
        [*The Ladies of Dante's Lyrics*, 137–138.]

This poem he sent "to many who were famous composers at that time," and answers came "from many people, and of different opinions; among which answerers was he whom I call the first of my friends, and he then wrote a sonnet which begins, 'All that is good, I think, hast thou beheld.' And this was almost the beginning of the friendship between him and me, when he learned that I was the one who had sent it to him." This "first friend" is Guido Cavalcanti, somewhat older than Dante and already a man of considerable note. His reply is preserved, as are two others: one by a minor poet named Dante da Maiano; one sometimes ascribed to a lad who later became a great jurist and a close friend of our author — Cino da Pistoia.

Now, when we look at Dante's verses, we find in them, first, the idea of a prophetic dream or vision,

which is too general to point to a definite model; it
may be Biblical or classical. Then we see the figure
of Love as a god, common in the Provençal poets,
who derived it in the first place from Ovid; Dante
probably knew it in both sources. From either,
or from both, he may have got the sad note at the
end — the expectation of sorrow from love. More
specific is the rather gruesome theme of a lady compelled to eat her lover's heart, a legend told in various quarters (not figuratively, as here, but literally),
and attached especially to the troubadour Guilhem
de Cabestaing. The figurative devouring of a heart
occurs also in a striking poem by Sordello, a famous
Italian who wrote in Provence, and who appears as
a noble figure in the *Divine Comedy*. Furthermore,
there is in the Bible (Revelation x, 10) a passage
that may have colored Dante's thought: "And I
took the little book out of the angel's hand, and ate
it up; and it was in my mouth sweet as honey: and
as soon as I had eaten it, my belly was bitter." The
little poem seems to indicate, then, familiarity with
Provençal verse, with the Bible, and perhaps with
Ovid. These Dante presumably knew; and he must
have known Virgil, the writer most studied in the
schools. There is more to be noted. Dante's poem
is a sonnet, a form unknown to the poets of southern
France, being an invention of the Sicilian School,
freely used, after the Sicilians, by the early songsters
of Tuscany and Bologna.

Furthermore, the sonnet by Dante and the re-
sponding sonnets of other authors form together
a composition termed in Provence *tenso*, in Italy
(where it was imitated by the earliest writers) *ten-
zone* or *contrasto*. It is a real or fictitious debate between two or more poets, in stanzas of the same
structure; among the Italians, the stanzas have always been sonnets. Here are a couple of strophes
of a Provençal *tenso* between the famous troubadour
Giraut de Bornelh and the scarcely less renowned
Count Raimbaut of Orange, nicknamed Linhaure,
on the respective merits of a clear and an obscure
style:

> Giraut de Bornelh, I would know
> Why you persistently refuse
> To praise th' obscure style poets use.
>   Now tell me why
>   You glorify
> A verse for which all men may care:
> Shall everybody have a share?
>
> My lord Linhaure, even so.
> 'T is right each one should have his views
> And suit himself, but my poor muse
>   Knows well that I
>   Am rated high
> When I the easiest verse prepare.
> To blame me, then, is hardly fair.
>   [*Dante*, 115–116.]

It may be noticed that the rimes in the two stanzas
are identical. This was regularly the case in Provençal, and often in Italian, where the practice of reply-

ing with the same rimes that were used by the first poet was called "rispondere per le rime."

As an example of a literary debate in early Italian we may take an exchange of sonnets between Bonagiunta Orbiciani of Lucca and Guido Guinizelli of Bologna, both of whom appear in the *Divine Comedy*, the first as an inquirer into the new style, the second as Dante's master in Italian verse.

BONAGIUNTA

Since you have found a novel way to write
   And changed the laws of our sweet amorous lays,
Both form and matter, turning black to white,
   Hoping thereby to win consummate praise,
I liken you unto a torch at night
   Which sheds a flickering gleam o'er murky ways,
But shines no longer when the orb of light
   Kindles the world with all-surpassing blaze.
Such subtle wit was never seen before:
   Your language is so hard to understand
     That not a reader can decipher it.
Altho' Bologna may beget such lore,
   It seems preposterous in any land
     To furnish poems forth from learned writ.

GUINIZELLI

The wise man runs not here and there at will,
   But stops and thinks, and measures in his mind;
And, having thought, he holds his thought until
   The truth assures him he has not been blind.
Let us beware lest pride our bosom fill;
   Let us consider our degree and kind.
Mad is the man who thinks the world sees ill
   And he alone is fit the truth to find.

All sorts of curious birds fly to and fro,
  Diverse in speed, unlike in temperament,
    And each conducts itself in its own wise.
God made a varied universe, and so
  Created understandings different —
    Which ought to make us slow to criticize.
                              [*Dante*, 118–119.]

These two poems, by the way, illustrate the type of sonnet that is probably earliest: two rimes alternating through the first eight lines; in the last six, three rimes, running *cde cde*.

For his sonnet-debate Dante had, then, abundant precedent in the literature of his century. His theme, however, was not a literary one: it was rather a discussion of Love — the favorite topic among the troubadours, who were apt to treat it in the more formal type of *tenso* known as *partimen* or *joc partit*, a debating game. There is a very good early Italian specimen, the participants being: Jacopo Mostacci; Pier delle Vigne, a sympathetic character in the *Commedia*, chancellor of the Emperor Frederick II; Giacomo da Lentini, leader of the Sicilian School, called by Dante (and often by himself) "the Notary." Sometimes the *tenso* ran into scurrilous abuse, as in a certain poetic dialogue between the popular troubadour Raimbaut de Vaqueiras and the Marquis Albert Malaspina, a member of a family that a century later entertained Dante. Although the tone of the poem is scandalous, the intention was probably comic. Such, too, I think, was the intent of a

sonnet-dialogue between Dante and his friend Bicci
Junior, or Forese Donati, a kinsman of the lady
whom Dante afterwards married. In the first sonnet, Dante makes fun of Bicci's wife and her contin-
ual colds, due to her husband's desertion; in the
second, Bicci tells how, at daybreak, he went out to
dig for hidden treasure in the graveyard and met
there the ghost of Dante's father. Then Dante
charges his friend with gluttony, which has brought
him to ruin. Bicci replies:

> Give back your borrowed clothing to St. Gall,
>   Before you sneer at other people's dress.
>   This winter many men are in distress,
> For you have fairly stript their hospital.
> And if our poverty is comical,
>   Please send to us for food a little less.
>   From Altafronte you get many a mess,
> Enough to stuff you like a cannibal.
> If you have Frank and Tana to support
>   (God give them health!) you shall have work to spare;
>   For with Belluzzo you have naught to do.
> Our hospital shall be your last resort:
>   I see you now in gay apparel there
>   At paupers' table, with the other two.

And Dante retorts:

> Bicci the Son (*whose* son, no one could say,
>   Unless his mother, Monna Tessa, could)
>   Has stowed away so much expensive food
> That other people's money has to pay.
> And men with gold about them will not stay,
>   Crying, when he comes nearer than he should:
>   "That fellow with the broken face is good
> At picking pockets; let us edge away!"

The man whom he calls father quakes in bed
  For fear his robber son may lose his life
    (His *son* no more than Christ was Joseph's child!).
Of Bicci and his brothers it is said,
  Each brings his booty to his brother's wife:
    Worthy descendants of a race defiled!

[*Dante*, 114-115.]

At the opposite extreme in sentiment is a *tenso* in two stanzas, by Dante, on the occasion of the death of Beatrice's father. This one is an example of the fictitious dialogue, in which both parts are written by the same author. The poet tells us that, as he was standing outside the house of mourning, he watched the passage of ladies who had been within, mourning with Beatrice; and, overhearing scraps of their conversation, he wove them into a speech supposed to be made by them in answer to an imaginary question by him:

DANTE TO LADIES

O ye who walk with self-forgetful mien,
  With lowered eyes betraying hidden rue,
  Whence come ye, wearing pity's very hue
And very look? Ah! tell, where have ye been?
Have ye perchance our gentle Lady seen,
  With Love upon her face all bathed in dew?
  Ladies, reply! My heart declares 't is true,
Because ye walk majestic, like a queen.
And if ye come from such a piteousness,
  I pray you here a bit with me to bide
And how it fares with her, to me confess.
  Your eyes cannot conceal that they have cried.
I see you come, such pictures of distress,
  I dare not think of what is prophesied.

Ladies to Dante

Art thou the man who oft hath been inclined
  To sing of Her, addressing us alone?
  His voice and thine, indeed, are like in tone,
And yet thy visage seems of different kind.
Alas! why weepest thou, so unresigned
  That thou wouldst kindle pity in a stone?
  Oh! hast thou listened to her piteous moan,
Who canst not now conceal thy sorrowing mind?
Leave tears to us, and sad funereal pace!
  'T is sin to wish that we be comforted,
Since we have heard her speak with mournful grace.
  Such sadness hovers plainly o'er her head
That who should try to look upon her face,
  Weeping would sink to earth before her, dead.
          [*The Ladies of Dante's Lyrics*, 115–116.]

Of the fictitious *tenso* we have some unmistakable
representatives in Provençal: one is a dialogue between a noble poet and his horse; another is a col-
loquy between a minstrel-monk and God.

On the mourning women and the death of the
father of Beatrice, Dante has left us two other sonnets: the first, "Whence come ye here so thoughtful
and so sad?" contains the poet's question, without
the answer; the second, "Ye ladies who your sympathy reveal," combines inquiry and reply in one
strophe. This theme brings us to another literary
type, the lament, called in Provençal *planh*, in Italian *compianto*. Among the poets of Provence, and
also among their Italian imitators, it dealt with the
death or departure of one's beloved or the death of a

patron or sovereign. The troubadours wrote several
fine elegies on the passing of Richard I of England;
the warlike Bertran de Born mourned over "the
young English King," eldest son of Henry II; an unknown poet deplored the loss of two young ladies
who had entered a convent; the death of Blacatz, a
noble patron of letters, called forth the best poem of
Sordello. One of the singers of the Sicilian group,
Giacomino Pugliese, has left us an elegy which begins thus:

Death, why dost thou afflict me with such pain,
  Stealing my love, and with her all my mirth?
The flower of earthly beauty hast thou slain;
  Now have I naught to live for, here on earth.
Discourteous Death, to treat my pleading so!
Thou 'st parted lovers, frozen pleasure's glow,
    Till all is sad.
My former gayety is turned to woe,
For thou hast killed all comfort here below,
    Which once I had.

Pleasure and sport and laughter once I knew
  Better by far than any other knight;
But when my lady forth to Heaven flew,
  Sweet hope went with her, and forsook me quite.
Grief have I still, and endless tears and sighs;
Society and sport and song and prize
    Are all forbid.
No more I see her at my coming rise,
No more she turns upon me her sweet eyes,
    As once she did.
            [*The Ladies of Dante's Lyrics*, 65–66.]

These Sicilian poets cultivated a special type of the *compianto:* the lamentation of a lady forsaken by her lover. This theme, known as the *donna abbandonata*, became very common in popular poetry, and, indeed, perhaps came originally from folk-song into the literary repertory. No doubt there was popular song of some kind in those early days; but, as it was not written down, we can only guess what it was like. That is why we cannot be sure, concerning certain themes, whether they originated with the unlettered rustics or with the courtly poets. The following example, by Odo delle Colonne, certainly suggests a strain of the people's muse. The woman speaks:

> Ah me! to love in vain!
>   Now tell once more, my song,
> Again and yet again,
>   How days and nights are long
> And life is naught but pain,
>   Tho' I have done no wrong.
>
> There 's one who 's all to me,
>   And he was mine before,
> But now he will not be.
>   Ah! who could suffer more!
> He treats me haughtily:
>   My heart is crusht and sore.
>
> Alas! what have I done?
>   Love will not let me go:
> His image lures me on,
>   Which hath enslaved me so.
> Since his fair face is gone,
>   No gladness do I know.

I hold no joy in fief;
    Love grants me only hate
And everlasting grief.
    O Death, be not too late!
Come now to my relief
    And save me from this state!

Ah me! why did he say,
    When no one else was nigh:
"Richly dost thou repay;
    Thy love's a prize so high,
I 'd not give it away
    For earth and stars and sky"?

And now (ingratitude!)
    He scorns me, and begins
On other thoughts to brood.
    O God! may she who wins
My love from her he wooed
    Perish with all her sins!

Go forth, my little song,
    To fortune's favored son;
And if he do me wrong,
    Strike him, the guilty one —
But not with blow too strong,
    Lest he be sore undone!

But strike and surely slay
    Her who usurps my place.
Then will he find his way
    To me, with smiling face,
Never again to stray.
    Joy will be mine, and grace!

A variant of the type is the plaint of a woman
whose lover has departed on a Crusade. Once, at
least, the theme was treated in Provençal, in a poem

by Marcabru. The Sicilians were successful in it, as may be seen from the following *compianto* by Rinaldo d'Aquino:

Sweetness is turned to canker
    And joy is turned to rue:
The ships are weighing anchor,
    They 'll soon be on the blue.
To Palestine he goeth,
    He goes, my lover true;
And I (how grieved, God knoweth!),
    Whatever shall I do?

The Cross should bring salvation,
    And me it but dismays;
The Cross brings desolation:
    I envy him who prays.
O pilgrim Cross, inhuman,
    (Alas! these wretched days!)
Why sacrifice poor woman?
    My heart is all ablaze!

The Emperor, they tell me,
    Keeps peace both far and near:
Then why should he compel me
    To yield what I hold dear?
O mighty God above me,
    Whom all the nations fear,
There is but one doth love me:
    O bring him safely here!

I 've told thee now, sweet poet,
    Whereof to make a lay;
Let all the singers know it,
    To Syria let it stray.
Sleep has forsook my pillow
    Nor can I rest by day:
To lands beyond the billow
    My life has fled away.

Dante and his group favored neither of these last two themes; they wrote *compianti* only on death. Here is one by Dante, in sonnet form, on the decease of a young friend of Beatrice:

Ye lovers, sigh! for Love, our Master, sighs.
  Now learn what grief hath banisht all his glee:
  Love heareth ladies calling piteously,
Their bitter pain revealing through their eyes.
Discourteous Death has set in cruel wise
  Upon a noble heart his stern decree,
  Destroying what in gentle ladies we,
Beside their good repute, on earth do prize.
What honor Love bestowed on her, now guess!
  I saw his very self lamenting there
    Over the charming form that lifeless lay,
    Lifting his mournful gaze to Heaven alway,
  Which had become the gentle soul's repair
That once was queen of all in joyousness.
                    [*The Ladies of Dante's Lyrics*, 66.]

Another poem by the same author on the same subject is full of conceits, and is written, also, in an expanded and difficult form of the sonnet known as the *sonetto rinterzato:*

O mean, ungentle Death, sweet pity's foe,
Old ancestor of woe,
  Inevitable sentence, and malign!
  Since thou hast stricken so this heart of mine
  That I must ever pine,
Blame thee I must, till tongue shall weary grow.
Would I make thee for mercy begging go,
To all the world I 'd show
  That one supremely sinful sin of thine;
  Not that the world hath seen thereof no sign,
  But rather to incline

To wrath all those the food of Love who know.
By thee our life is robbed of courtesy
  And all the goodness we to woman trace;
  Youth's joyous face
Hath lost its loving charm because of thee.
I will not tell who may this lady be,
  Save by her virtues known in every place.
  Unless one merit grace,
One never must expect such company.
                    [*The Ladies of Dante's Lyrics*, 63–64.]

In the sixty years or so that intervened between
the invention of the sonnet and Dante's first use of
it, the form had undergone many variations; and it
is noteworthy that our poet, after his earliest period,
should have preferred the simpler, more primitive
types, of fourteen lines. Of the first four sonnets in
the *New Life*, two are *sonetti rinterzati;* but we never
find in the little book this intricate variety again.
Several elegies in plain sonnet form Dante wrote on
the death of his Beatrice, and one in the form of a
canzone, or ode, "My eyes in sorrow for my heart's
distress." Here is one stanza of this last poem:

Hard and distressful comes my sighing breath
  When thought recalleth to my heavy mind
    The vanisht one by whom my heart was cleft;
And oftentimes, as I reflect on death,
  So sweetly to its charm am I inclined,
    I yearn until I have no color left.
    And when her image seeks my soul bereft,
  Such pain on every hand assails me then,
    I shiver at the agonizing blow;
    My spirit sinks so low,
For very shame I shun the sight of men.

> Then, weeping, in my solitary woe
> I call on Beatrice: "Canst thou be dead!"
> And while I call on her, am comforted.

It closes with this envoy:

> My piteous song, now go thy way in grief!
> The maids and ladies find, on whom, in state,
> Thy sisters used to wait,
> With messages that always spake of gladness;
> And thou, the youngest daughter, child of sadness,
> Go forth to dwell with them, disconsolate.

A sonnet, and also a short *canzone*, of only two stanzas, "Alas! whenever I recall to mind," Dante wrote — so he tells us — at the request of a friend, a brother of his beloved, really for Beatrice, but ostensibly on the death of another lady. The sonnet, *Venite a intender li sospiri miei*, runs thus:

> O come and hear me utter sigh on sigh,
> Ye gentle hearts, for pity wills it so!
> O hear my sighs, which melancholy go!
> And but for them of sorrow I should die;
> Because my eyes, however hard they try,
> Could never pay their heavy debt of woe,
> Mourning my love with such an endless flow
> My heart were eased, tho' I should weep them dry.
> Full often shall ye hear my sighs extol
> My gentle love, who hath her wings unfurled
> To seek the Heaven her virtue hath deserved;
> And ye shall hear them oft condemn this world,
> As doth my stricken, solitary soul,
> Forsaken by the blessed power it served.

Another *compianto* on the loss of Beatrice was written by Dante's friend, Cino da Pistoia, who

composed one also on the death of the Emperor,
Henry VII, whom Dante so admired.

But enough has been said to show how Dante
selected and adapted to his purpose two of the conventional types of Provençal and early Italian literature: the *tenso*, or discussion, and the *planh*, or
elegy. The former he used for amatory, funereal,
and humorous themes; the latter he restricted to one
function — lamentation over the death of a lady.
What were the other lyric themes and forms current
in the literature of southern France? The *balada*, or
ballad, — a dance-song actually performed by danc-
ing ladies, — usually treated, in Provence, some
light or realistic love theme; Dante made it the
vehicle of delicate sentiment and dainty conceits, as
in this little poem:

CHORUS

Ah! Violet, which once didst meet mine eyes,
  Shadowed by Love, appearing suddenly,
  Pity the heart which wounded was by thee,
Which hopes in thee, and, yearning for thee, dies.

SOLO

Thou, Violet, in beauty past belief,
With fatal words didst kindle in my mind
  A furious fire, the while
Thou, like a blazing spirit swift and kind,
Didst fashion hope, which partly cures my grief,
  Whene'er I see thee smile.
  Ah! scorn me not, tho' I myself beguile!
  Think of the longings which within me burn!
  For many a bygone maid, tho' slow to turn,
Hath felt at last the pain she did despise.

CHORUS

Ah! Violet, which once didst meet mine eyes,
  Shadowed by Love, appearing suddenly,
  Pity the heart which wounded was by thee,
Which hopes in thee, and, yearning for thee, dies.
              [*The Ladies of Dante's Lyrics*, 4.]

For the serious expression of love the poets of the
Midi had the *canso*, their principal lyric form, which
in Italian was called *canzone*. Of course there is
much variety in elaborating the theme; but we may
say, in general, that the Provençal conception of it
is feudal — the lady being regarded as a superior,
an absolute sovereign, the lover as a vassal. This
convention was ordinarily followed by the earliest
Italian amatory poets. But with Guido Guinizelli
of Bologna there came a change: with him, the conception of love is no longer feudal, but religious.
The lady is still a superior, but not an earthly one:
she becomes a symbol of the angelic nature, the
heavenly intelligence; and the lover exchanges the
position of vassal for that of worshiper. This atti-
tude may be illustrated by a stanza from Dante's
first *canzone* in the "sweet new style" — "Ladies
who have intelligence of love":

My lady's longed for in the heavens above.
  Now let me tell you of her wondrous might.
  Whatever lady would be "gentle" hight
    Should walk with her; for when she goes her way,
A chill is cast on vulgar hearts by Love,
  And all their thoughts are cold and dead with fright.

> Whoe'er should stand his ground to see the sight
>   Would be ennobled or would turn to clay.
>   When she discerns a worthy man who may
> Rightly behold her, he must own her power;
> For blessedness she gives, a mystic dower,
>   So humbling him, no spite can with him stay.
> God granteth her a grace that's greater still:
> Who speaks to her, escapes eternal ill.
>   [*The Ladies of Dante's Lyrics*, 21–22.]

Not all of Dante's amatory poetry is in this vein. In fact, an interesting passage in the *New Life* tells of his conversion. His previous style differs not only in its more worldly conception of the lady, but also in the prominence of the author's self:

> Of Love within me speaketh every thought;
>   And yet they show so much variety
>   That one doth make me crave his tyranny,
> Another reckons all his power as naught,
> Another, hopeful, sweetness may have brought,
>   Another makes me weep full frequently.
>   Only agreed in asking sympathy,
> They quake with fear, by which the heart is caught.
> And therefore, doubting which my theme shall be,
>   I fain would write, but know not what to say,
>   And thus in Love's bewildering maze am lost.
>   Would I agreement have, at any cost,
>   Mine enemy I needs must call and pray:
>   "My lady Pity, come and comfort me!"
>   [*The Ladies of Dante's Lyrics*, 26.]

Often enough the Provençal and the Sicilian *canso* was frankly passionate; and so are a few of Dante's *canzoni* — particularly some of those connected with Pietra — but apparently none of those associated with Beatrice. Two conventional figures of the old *canso* — the jealous husband and the informer — are absent from Dante.

No material or trivial details are to be found in his odes, which keep themselves in the realm of the abstract. In one poem (a *serventese*), unfortunately lost but mentioned in the *New Life*, he did enumerate "the sixty most beautiful ladies" of Florence; what his treatment of the topic was, we do not know. Possibly it was suggested to him by a *canso* of Raimbaut de Vaqueiras, the "Chariot." This poem tells how all the ladies, jealous of a certain Beatrice, resolve to wage war upon her, but are ignominiously defeated; and there is a long list of the belligerent ladies. A similar enumeration occurs in the "Truce" by Guilhem de la Tor. Another Provençal *canso* may have suggested to Dante a theme of a different type: Giraut de Bornelh relates that, following the song of a bird, he comes upon three damsels weeping, who deplore with him the depravity of the times. Similarly, Dante hears three ladies mourning over the degeneracy of the present day; but Dante's ladies are allegorical.

Next to the *canso*, among Provençal forms, may be placed the *sirventes*, a satirical or polemical or abusive poem written to an old tune. Some of the most spirited of them dealt with war. Here is a strophe of one by Raimbaut de Vaqueiras, composed after he had received knighthood from Boniface, Marquis of

Monferrat, whom he accompanied on the fourth
Crusade to Constantinople:

> Gallop and trot and leap and run,
> Night-watch and labor and distress
> Henceforth shall be my business;
> Cold I'll endure, and scorching sun.
> Iron and staff and steel my arms shall be,
> And forest-paths shall be my hostelry.
> Discord and *sirventes* shall be my song,
> While I maintain the weak against the strong.
>   [*Dante*, 108.]

Although Dante became familiar with Bertran de
Born, the best representative of this type, he has left
us nothing formally of the Provençal *sirventes* class.
Three of his poems, however, belong in theme to this
category rather than to that of the *canso;* they are:
the third *canzone* of the *Convivio*, "The dulcet rimes
of love which I was used," a versified disquisition on
nobility; the ode "'T is grief emboldens now my
heart to speak," a diatribe against the vices of men,
particularly avarice; and "Since Love hath utterly
forsaken me," a demonstration that true grace cannot exist without virtue and love.

The other Provençal lyric types apparently did
not appeal to Dante — such as the *pastorela*, a conversation between the poet and a country girl; the
alba, or dawn-song; the *enueg* and *plazer*, enumera-
tions of things one dislikes and likes. Nor did he
imitate the *ensenhamen*, a versified set of rules for
conduct, nor any other kind of didactic poem in

rimed couplets, nor the epistle constructed on the same plan. Nor, in all probability, the *descort* and the *lais*, written in several languages or in irregular metres. Out of all the forms that southern France had to offer, Dante selected three: the *canso*, vehicle of exalted emotion, one variety of which is the *planh*, or elegy; the *balada*, light song of amatory fancies; the *tenso*, or poetic dialogue. And he made abundant use of that new Italian type, the sonnet, a convenient medium, which could be used for almost any purpose.

By the time Dante was twenty-eight or twenty-nine years old, and was constructing the *New Life* (picking out and arranging the poems, and writing the prose), he had extended his acquaintance with letters. Of the Latin poets, he had added Lucan and Horace (that is, the Horace of the *Poetics*) to Virgil and Ovid. He had studied the *Consolation of Philosophy* by Boethius, and Cicero's treatise *On Friendship* — perhaps more of Cicero's philosophical works. He had plunged into the theologians, especially St. Thomas Aquinas. Undoubtedly he had enlarged his knowledge of vernacular literature, perhaps taking in some French as well as more Provençal. His education did not stop there. Ten years or so later, when he came to write the *Banquet*, he was not only an expert in scholastic philosophy and astronomical and physical science, but also a good Latinist, acquainted with the philosophy of Cicero and

Seneca, the history of Livy and Paulus Orosius. If we pass on ten or fifteen years more, to the period when Dante, some forty or forty-five years old, was engaged on the final redaction of the *Divine Comedy*, we find that he has further increased his store of theology and of medieval philosophy and science, and has added also some ancient Latin authors, such as Pliny, Solinus, Valerius Maximus, and especially the epic poet Statius. Most of Aristotle he acquired, first through St. Thomas, then directly in a Latin version; and a little of Plato he found translated. He never learned Greek or Hebrew, except a few words picked up from his authorities; and he gives no indication of acquaintance with Spanish, German, or English.

The expansion of his horizon by this long-continued and intense study could not fail to offer new possibilities in the way of themes and treatment. In St. Thomas Aquinas he came upon a definition of the theory of allegory, as well as the application of it to Biblical interpretation. And Boethius's *Consolation of Philosophy* furnished him with the figure of Philosophy symbolized as a majestic lady. Hence, no doubt, came the suggestion of Dante's lyrics in honor of Lady Philosophy, which were written, it would seem, just after the period of the *Vita Nuova*. As to the *Vita Nuova*, or *New Life*, a sort of spiritual autobiography in the form of a continuous commentary on thirty-one of the author's poems, Dante seems to have got the idea of that structure from some Provençal song-book — probably an edition of Bertran de Born wherein the lyrics are accompanied by a prose explanation which relates the career of the poet. The style of the prose, in the *New Life*, is distinctly flavored with the language of the Bible. The analyses of the poems show the influence of St. Thomas's commentary on Aristotle. For the *Banquet*, Dante adopted the general plan that he had used to such advantage in the *New Life:* a discussion of some of his own lyrics; but here the proportion of prose to verse is far greater than in the earlier work. Boethius's *Consolation of Philosophy* afforded him an example of an extended philosophical treatise interspersed with poetry. In style and in method of exposition Dante followed scholastic Latin models. So he naturally did, also, in his three didactic Latin works: the broadly planned but unfinished book *On Vernacular Composition;* the compact and well-rounded argument on *Monarchy;* the scientific lecture on the *Problem of Water and Land*. The last two dealt with questions debated in his day; but the first, the *Vernacular Composition*, struck out in a new direction. Horace's *Ars Poetica* (Aristotle's *Poetics* was unknown) had to do with a very different kind of literature; the Rhetorics of Aristotle and Cicero scarcely touched upon Dante's theme; the linguistic treatises, in the language of southern France, known as the *Provençal Donatus* and the

Explanation of Verse-Making, merely grazed the subject; the big Provençal compendium of the art of versification, the *Laws of Love*, was not yet written. In this work, then, Dante showed himself an original investigator and a pioneer.

Our author has left us also some letters on various subjects, mostly political; one, however, is a message of condolence, one a little introduction (apparently) to a *canzone*, and one (if it be his) accompanied the first canto of the *Paradiso* sent to Can Grande della Scala. This last, which is really a treatise of some length, deals with allegory, composition, and rhetoric. In these epistles — Cicero's letters being still inaccessible — Dante followed the medieval style, with its pedantic language, violent figures, and rhythmical cadences. He contrived, nevertheless, to put into them something of his own. Two Latin eclogues complete the list of his Latin works; these have to do with personal matters — his preference for Italian and his use of it in his great poem, and his reluctance to leave Ravenna to visit Bologna, whither he was invited. The style is highly figurative and allegorical, so much so that it is hard to tell what the author is talking about. His method is based evidently on a study of Virgil's eclogues as they were interpreted in his day: namely, as poems fundamentally and intricately symbolistic.

We come now to Dante's great poem, the *Divine Comedy*, the book which he knew to be his masterpiece, the crowning achievement of his life, his title to immortality among men. Apparently he intended, from the beginning, that his chief work should be a monument to the memory of Beatrice; for at the close of the *New Life*, after describing in a sonnet the glory of his lady in Heaven, he proceeds to say: "After this sonnet there appeared to me a wondrous vision, in which I saw things that made me determine to write no more of this blessed one until I should be able to treat of her more worthily. And to that end I am studying with all my might, as she truly knows. Wherefore, if it shall be the pleasure of Him by whom all things live, that my life endure for some years, I hope to say of her what never was said of any woman." It is (let us say) the year 1294; the place is Florence. Here we have a man twenty-nine years old, of considerable reading, who has won distinction as a lyric poet, and who feels himself capable of far higher flights in literature. What theme shall be chosen by such a man? What theme is best adapted to satisfy his own artistic ambition and to perpetuate the name of his beloved, now a blessed soul in Paradise? What was the "wondrous vision" that flashed upon him, after he had composed the last sonnet of the *New Life*?

Some there are who think that Dante had selected his subject years before, when he wrote "Ladies who have intelligence of love," the first ode of the *New*

Life, and the first poem of any kind after his conversion to platonic love and the "sweet new style." Now there is some ground for believing that he composed this *canzone* when he was about twenty-two or twenty-three. The second stanza of the ode runs as follows:

> An angel in the mind of God doth call,
>   Saying: "O Lord, on earth there meets our eyes
>   A wondrous virtue which doth hither rise
>   Forth from a soul whose light doth climb anear."
> And Paradise, which lacketh naught at all
>   Save only her, unto its Maker cries —
>   And every saint — to bring her to the skies.
>   Pity alone our earthly plea doth hear;
>   For God declareth of my Lady dear:
> "In peace, beloved spirits, suffer still
> That she for whom ye hope await my will
>   Below, where some one her release doth fear,
>   One who shall say in Hell: 'O souls distrest,
>   Mine eyes have seen the hope of all the blest.'"

> E che dirà nell' Inferno: O malnati,
> Io vidi la speranza de' beati.
>   [*The Power of Dante*, 192.]

At first sight, one would infer that the writer of these lines had already conceived the plan of a mystic journey through the world of the dead. If so, he radically altered his design; for, in point of fact, in the *Divine Comedy*, he never mentions Beatrice in Hell. Supposing Dante had never written the *Commedia*, the closing verses of our strophe would naturally be understood as meaning simply that the poet

(for I take the "some one" to refer to him) will proclaim his lady's name to the ends of the universe,
even to the depths of Hell. The poem is couched in
a vein of supreme hyperbole: Heaven is incomplete
without Beatrice, the angels are clamoring for her;
her virtue awakens admiration on high; Dante, who
knows she is too pure for this world, will sound her
praises down below. We need not assume any real
apprehension of an early death for Beatrice —
merely the general idea that earth does not deserve
to keep her. Still less need we understand (as some
have done) that Dante expects to be damned; indeed, that possibility is precluded by the closing
lines of the next stanza:

> God granteth her a grace that 's greater still:
> Who speaks to her, escapes eternal ill.

Whether Dante, before the time indicated in the
last chapter of the *New Life*, had any design of
a supreme literary undertaking, remains, then, I
think, an open question. Had he a plan or not, various possibilities were before him. Let us assume
that, being a poet, he would inevitably make his
masterpiece a poem. In northern France there were
fine epics of war and chivalry, some of the stories of
which, at least, had reached Italy. Dante knew the
romance of *Lancelot of the Lake*, the book which
Paolo and Francesca read together; in his *Hell* he
refers to the blow of King Arthur which slew the
traitorous Mordrec; and in his *Paradise* he com-

pares the indulgently rebuking smile of Beatrice to the protesting cough of the Lady of Mallehault, at the interview of Lancelot and Guinivere. He knew Tristan as a great lover. He knew Achilles in the same rôle, and that hero's tragic end, as told in the Old French romance of Troy. The *Aliscans* he knew, the epic of William of Orange. And he knew how Roland blew his horn at Roncevaux. In *De Vulgari Eloquentia* he speaks of French as the language of "histories of the Trojans and Romans and the charming divagations of King Arthur." But he chose none of these themes. The epics and romances of southern France were probably unknown to him, but they would hardly have appealed to him more than those of the north.

In northern France, in the thirteenth century, was produced that wonderfully popular allegorical, satirical, and didactic poem, the *Romance of the Rose*, at least the first part of which was known to his elderly adviser, Brunetto Latini, who had lived in Paris. But whether Dante himself knew it, save by report, we cannot say. In his surely authentic works there is no trace of it, unless the white rose of his Paradise be intended as a counterpart of the red rose of the French romance. On the other hand, there was made, in his own time, an Italian abridged paraphrase of the poem, in the form of a sonnet sequence, of such admirable workmanship that some have attributed it to Dante himself. At any rate, he

did not select a similar theme for his masterpiece.
With the drama, religious and secular, which had
developed in France, he shows no acquaintance; nor
was he acquainted, it would seem, with the *Romance of Reynard the Fox;* nor with the pretty tale
of *Aucassin and Nicolette.* Nothing that he knew
in French literature prompted him to imitation,
and no work on a large scale in the literature of
Provence.

This being the case, he might conceivably have
turned to Latin. Petrarch, a generation later, based
his chief hope of fame on a Latin epic, the *Africa,*
dealing with Scipio Africanus. Dante, too, might
have attempted a history in "grammatical" verse,
on the pattern of Virgil or Lucan. Possibly — since
he perhaps had read some of Seneca's plays — he
might, like his contemporary and fellow-countryman Mussato, have tried his hand at a Latin tragedy. But his ambition lay in another direction.
Had he known them, some of the late and medieval
Latin poets — the allegorical ones — might have
offered him a more congenial model: Prudentius,
with his *Soul's Battle;* or Alanus de Insulis, with his
Anticlaudian and his *Nature's Lament.* For Dante
loved allegory, and his bent was strongly religious
and didactic. His didactic impulse, so manifest in
the *Banquet,* led him to explore encyclopedic works,
from Pliny through St. Isidore to the *Treasure* of his
elderly friend, Brunetto Latini.

Now this same Brunetto, who, after a sojourn in France, spent the latter part of his life in his native Florence, where he was a very prominent citizen, wrote not only his *Treasure* in French prose (one of the most highly prized of all encyclopedias), but also a little *Treasure* in Italian verse, which was a combination of instruction and allegory, and was worked out, furthermore, in the form of a journey. Lost in a strange wood, the author, coming to his senses, encounters the beauteous Dame Nature, who bestows on him much precious information. After traversing a wilderness, he reaches the Land of Virtue; but, not content, he pushes on to the Land of Pleasure, where he falls under the dominion of Love, whose code is there expounded. Snatched from danger by Ovid, purified by penance, he goes back to the wood in search of the Liberal Arts. Many countries he crosses, never stopping until he rides to the top of Mt. Olympus, where he meets the venerable sage, Ptolemy. Here the narrative breaks off. It is not a high flight of poetry, but it is ingenious, and it imparts valuable knowledge under the cloak of an allegorical journey. In this poem, the *Tesoretto*, we probably have one of the first models for the *Divine Comedy*. Dante was certainly conscious of a great debt to Latini, whose soul he meets in Hell. "You, Master Brunetto, here!" he exclaims.

And he replied: "Be not displeased, my son,
    If old Latini follows thee a bit,
    And backward turns, and lets the band go on."

    .   .   .   .

"If favoring Heaven on all my wishes smiled,"
    I answered him, "I earnestly would pray
    You were not yet from human life exiled.
For memory, now a sorrow, keeps alway
    Your kindly image, dear and fatherly,
    When in the world above, from day to day,
You taught me how to win eternity.
    How great my gratitude, while I shall live,
    'T is meet my words make all mankind to see."
                                        [*Dante*, 267–268.]

Other journeys, legendary or symbolical, Dante
must have drawn upon, particularly expeditions to
the Earthly Paradise — such as the tale of three
monks who found the Garden of Eden at the top of
a mountain a hundred miles high, or the famous
Navigation of the Irish monk, St. Brendan, who discovered the Isle of the Blest. From a different kind
of legend Dante derived far more — the story of
visions of the other world. Of these there were
many, from the fourth-century Apocalypse of St.
Paul down to Dante's own time. From them, and
also from Virgil, he got many details for his *Hell*;
but the logical arrangement of it is his own invention.

The vision, the journey, the compendium of
knowledge — all these types are fused together and
invested with allegory. But we have not yet found

the real spirit, the soul of Dante's theme. The *Divine Comedy*, like the *New Life*, is first and foremost a psychic autobiography; it is a record of awakening from sin, of remorse, of reformation, of discipline, of purification, of religious contemplation, and of union of the soul with God. Had Dante a model for a work of this nature? He had; and he names it in his *Banquet*, in the passage which states the conditions under which it is legitimate to speak of one's self. "The second," he says, "is when, by talking of one's self, very great assistance is rendered to others in the way of teaching. And this reason impelled St. Augustine to speak of himself in his *Confessions;* for in the progress of his life, which was from bad to good, from good to better, and from better to best, he has given us an example and a lesson, which else could not have been had from so true a witness."

Inwardly a spiritual confession, outwardly an allegorical journey in the form of a vision, with much incidental doctrine, the *Commedia* blends these several types into one, and a new theme is created — a theme which the poet clothes with all the splendors of language and imagination. Truthfully could Dante say, in his *Paradise:*

> L' acqua che io prendo giammai non si corse.

Chapter VIII

DANTE'S VERSE

IN the Limbus, the afterworld of the virtuous heathen, Dante sees a great light shining in the darkness, and, illumined by it, certain shades, whose dignified bearing sets them apart from their fellows. Wondering, he turns to Virgil, who has guided him thither; and, in answer to his inquiry,

> Virgil replied to me: "Their honored name,
>   Which still reëchoes in the world of men,
>   Wins heavenly grace which thus preserves their fame."
> A sudden voice I heard exclaiming then:
>   "Honor the noble poet, now be glad!
>   His shade, which left us, cometh back again."
> When silent was the voice which welcome bade,
>   I four majestic shades advancing see,
>   Whose faces neither joyous are nor sad.
> And thus my kindly Master spake to me:
>   "Look well on him who cometh sword in hand,
>   And kinglike walks before the other three;
> Homer is this, who poets doth command.
>   Horace the satirist is second there.
>   The third is Ovid. Lucan ends the band.
> Since every one of these with me doth share
>   The title which the single voice doth call,
>   They do me honor, as is right and fair."
> Thus I beheld united, grand and tall,
>   Those princes of the most exalted song
>   Which like an eagle flieth over all.

Before their greetings had extended long,
    They turned to me with hospitable sign;
    And Virgil smiled, assured they did no wrong.
But, thanks to them, more glory still was mine;
    For they received me in their company,
    And I was sixth in that enlightened line.
                            [*Inf.*, IV, 76–102:
                translation from *The Power of Dante*, 78–79.]

Dante knew — he could not help knowing — that
his place was among the greatest poets of earth. Far
from boastful, his self-appreciation is over-modest,
for he assigns himself the sixth and last place,
whereas posterity has generally awarded him the
first. What gave him this high station? First of all,
his genius, which, in his belief, was due to the stars
that presided over his birth. He came into the
world between May 21 and June 21, when the sun
is in the sign of the Twins, and this constellation of
Gemini, the house of Mercury, bestows the gift of
literary art. When, in his mystic journey, Dante
reaches the heaven of the fixed stars, he finds himself in Gemini, his native constellation; and of the
luminaries that compose it he implores skill to complete his arduous task.

            O glorious stars, O light that ever teems
                With wondrous power, to which alone I owe
                My genius (or the thing that genius seems),
            The sun, begetter of the life below,
                Did daily set with you and daily rise
                When first I felt the Tuscan breezes blow.
            And then when Grace allotted me the prize
                Of penetrating your revolving wheel,
                Your region was assigned me in the skies.

> To you devoutly doth my soul appeal
>> For vigor now to meet the trial-time
>> Whose near approach I apprehensive feel.
>>>> [*Par.*, xxii, 112–123.]

Not only the natural operation of the stars but a special, mysterious grace of God had conferred on the poet, at his birth, a disposition for high achievement. In the Garden of Eden the soul of Beatrice, complaining to the angels of Dante's misuse of his gift, speaks as follows:

> Not merely from the wheeling of the spheres,
>> Which every seed to its fulfilment send
>> According as the starry sky appears,
> But through the gift of grace that knows no end,
>> Which raineth down from such a hidden height
>> That human power the veil can never rend,
> This man's new life possest such mental sight,
>> Potentially, that every goodly art
>> Its uttermost in him had brought to light.
>>>> [*Purg.*, xxx, 109–117.]

Natural disposition, however, does not suffice unless it be cultivated by study, properly directed. An arduous and indefatigable student was Dante. In his odes conceived in honor of Lady Philosophy, but composed in the form of amatory poems, Love (he tells us in his commentary) stands for the *study* expended by the author in winning the favor of his mistress. At the close of the *New Life*, he declares, referring to the sonnet that describes the ascent of his thought to Beatrice in Heaven: "After this sonnet there appeared to me a wondrous vision, in

which I saw things which made me determine to
write no more of this blessed lady until such time as
I should be able to treat of her more worthily. And
to this end I am *studying* with all my might, as she
truly knows."

Theology, philosophy, almost all accessible science and literature formed the subject of Dante's
study. Earlier, perhaps, than the sterner sciences,
the craft of versification attracted him, and he
worked it out from the poems of his predecessors.
This is the branch of study that immediately interests us. With it, no doubt, went music. In later life
Dante began a learned Latin treatise on the theme,
the *De Vulgari Eloquentia;* but he had mastered the
lesson before he was eighteen. Just previous to the
first piece of verse in the *New Life* occurs this sentence: "Meditating over what had appeared to me,
I resolved to make it heard by many who were
famous composers of that day; and inasmuch as I
had already *found out by myself* the art of writing
words in rime, I resolved to make a sonnet."

In prosody, then, Dante had no teacher; he
studied it alone, dissecting the lyrics of the Provençal troubadours, those of the so-called Sicilians as
well, and the more recent songs of Tuscany and
Bologna. Among the poets of the university city,
the one he rated highest, and therefore (we may conjecture) studied most assiduously, was Guido Guinizelli, whom he calls "my father and the father of

others, my betters, who ever wrote sweet rimes of love." When Dante meets Guido's soul in Purgatory, he walks for a long time gazing at it, without speech or hearing.

When I had fed my eyes upon the wraith,
    I begged to do him service, as a grace,
    With protestations such as capture faith.
And he to me: "Thy words have left a trace
    Upon my memory, a trace so clear
    That Lethe cannot blur it, nor efface.
But name the reason why thou dost appear
    (If all thy vows have told the truth to me)
    In word, and in thy look, to hold me dear."
And I to him: "Your dulcet poesy,
    Whose cherisht ink nor men nor time shall mar,
    Until our modern tongue shall cease to be."
                            [*Purg.*, xxvi, 103–114:
                            translation from *Dante*, 94.]

Three other poets of Bologna are cited by our author in his *De Vulgari Eloquentia*. Of the Tuscans who wrote before his own time, two receive significant mention in the *Divine Comedy:* Bonagiunta of Lucca and Guittone of Arezzo. The ghost of Bonagiunta addresses Dante in Purgatory, in the familiar passage that gave currency to the phrase *dolce stil nuovo:*

"Do I behold that poet here above
    Who publisht, down below, the novel screed,
    Ladies who have intelligence of love?"
And I to him: "A man am I who heed
    What Love dictates within, and copy plain
    The lessons his inspiring voice doth read."

"O brother, now I see," quoth he, "the chain
  Which bound the Notary, Guittone, me,
  Who never could that sweet new style attain.
Your close-pursuing pens I clearly see,
  Attentive to the voice that leads before —
  Which surely never did befall us three.
And one who ponders deep the problem o'er,
  Naught else shall find 'twixt one and t' other style."
  And, satisfied with that, he said no more.
                    [*Purg.*, XXIV, 49–63:
                    translation from *Dante*, 136–137.]

The Guittone named by Bonagiunta is the Guittone
of Arezzo just mentioned, the most prominent poet
of the early Tuscans. The Notary cited with Guittone is Giacomo da Lentini, leader of the Sicilian
School. Two other Sicilians are cited in *De Vulgari
Eloquentia*, and one more, Pier delle Vigne, is a
striking and pathetic figure in Dante's *Inferno*.

The versification of all these Italians is not essentially different from that of the Provençal troubadours whom they imitated, and to whom, no doubt,
Dante went for his first information. A considerable
number of them appear in his Latin treatise, quoted
side by side with the Italians; and one of them, Arnaut Daniel, is held up in the *Divina Commedia* as
the greatest of all poets in the vulgar tongue. He
appears in Purgatory, beside Guido Guinizelli, and
this high appreciation of him is put into the mouth
of the latter, who is still addressing Dante:

"Brother, my finger points ahead, not far,
  To one," he pointing said, "who merits more,
  A better forger of vernacular.

Love-verses, prose romance, all written lore
  Did he surpass. Let fools recite their part
  Who place the bard of Limousin before.
Report, not truth, impels the foolish heart;
  And so the fool doth lock his judgment fast
  Before he lists to reason or to art.
Thus many praised Guittone in the past,
  From mouth to mouth extolling only him.
  But truth has triumpht, more than once, at last."
                    [*Purg.*, XXVI, 115–126:
                    translation from *Dante*, 94.]

Arnaut himself then comes into sight, and, in reply
to the author's polite inquiry, addresses him in the
tongue of his own southern France. These eight
lines of Provençal, manifestly composed by Dante
himself for his Provençal character, may be regarded
as a tribute, an evidence of proficiency, offered by
the disciple to the master from whose writings the
pupil had acquired knowledge both of their language and of their technique. Nowhere else in the
Commedia are Dante's foreign or ancient personages
really made to employ their own idiom. Thus Arnaut speaks, amid the cleansing flames of Purgatory:

Unurged by prayer, his answer promptly came:
  "Your courteous request delights me so,
  I cannot, will not hide from you my name.
Arnaut am I, who weeping, singing go;
  My foolish past with tears I contemplate,
  But joyously await the noonday glow.
Now you by Heaven's power I supplicate, —
  Which up the stairway leads you ever higher, —
  While yet 't is time, be mindful of my fate."
Then vanisht in the purifying fire.
                    [*Purg.*, XXVI, 140–148.]

The supreme position accorded Arnaut — a place above all other prose or verse writers in any vernacular — testifies, in itself, to the labor Dante had spent upon him, and to the profit he had derived from his toil. For nothing in Arnaut's writing justifies such praise. He is, to be sure, an admirable craftsman, clever, ingenious, and difficult beyond his fellows, bewildering in the abundance and intricacy of his rimes; but of poetic feeling he shows little evidence. It is characteristic of Dante that he should have chosen for his textbook, so to speak, the hardest, the most impenetrable of the available models. He believed that the poet, though *born* with the gift, must be *made* by strenuous discipline. In this he agreed with Petrarch, who once wrote of his friend Rienzi: "This man has never composed a single genuine poem which has reached my ears, nor has he applied himself to such a task; and without application nothing, however easy, can be well done." Characteristic of our author, too, is the enthusiastic gratitude which prompted him to exaggerate almost fantastically the merits of one to whom he felt himself indebted. For Virgil, to whom he was under still greater obligations, he conceived a love and reverence, a devoted fellowship such as one seldom bears even to a living comrade and teacher. To Donatus, the author of his Latin grammar, he assigned a post in Heaven among the lights of theology.

Virgil and Arnaut Daniel represented, of course, to Dante as they do to us, not only two widely diverse languages but also two quite different systems of versification. Virgil wrote in *grammatica*, Arnaut in *volgare*. If Dante got from the former his conception of the *bello stile*, he had recourse to the latter for metrical technique. The Latin poets wrote *verse*, in which the chief ingredient is measure, a fixed though more or less flexible pattern of long and short syllables. The vernacular songsters composed *rimes*, that is, poems in which the principal factor is identity of sound at the end of the lines. This vernacular poetry, instead of counting quantities, counted syllables, and substituted for a regulated scheme of accents, with one dominant beat to each bar, a concentration of energy on the close of each line, this emphasis being enhanced by rime. If the line was long, there was another strong stress in the middle. The other syllables are arranged without much concern for rhythmic alternation of strong and weak. For instance, Bernart de Ventadorn begins thus his famous song on the lark:

> Quan vei la lauzeta movér
>   De ioi sas alas contra l rái,
> Que s'oblida e s laissa cazér
>   Per la doussor qu' al cor li vái . . .

Thus, in his partly Bolognese Italian, writes Guido Guinizelli:

Passa per via adorna e sì gentíle
Che sbassa argoglio a cui dona salúte
E fa 'l de nostra fe se no la créde;
E non si po apressare omo ch' è víle.
Ancor ve dico c' ha mazor vertúte:
Nul om po mal pensar fin che la véde.

As an example of a long line with a stress and a pause in the interior, we may take the beginning of the Old Provençal *Boeci*, or *Boethius:*

Nos jove ómne,   quandius qu'e nos estám,
De grant follía   per foll' edat parllám.

For Italian we may cite the opening of a famous burlesque poem in a Neapolitan dialect:

Rosa fresc' aulentíssima   ch'appar in ver l'estáte,
Le donne ti disíano,   pulzell' e maritáte.
Traggimi d'esta fócora   se t'est'a a bolontáte.

How this Romance verse, which ignores quantity, counts syllables, and marks lines by rime at the end — how this verse arose, no one can tell. We find it in substantially identical form at the beginning of the literatures of France, Italy, and Spain. It seems to have developed in the main from Latin hymns and sequences, the hymn being a song in rhythmic, often rimed verse, the sequence originally a piece of prose set to music. These compositions, being carried by the Church into all Christendom, produced in the various Christian countries analogous results. Some local differences are due to diversities in language. Provençal is a speech made up chiefly

of monosyllables and words stressed on the last
syllable; hence rimes are, as in English, prevailingly
monosyllabic.

> Pus de chantar m'es pres taléns,
> Farai un vers don sui doléns:
> No serai mais obediéns
> En Peytau ni en Lemozí.

The masculine line — that is, the line accented on
the last syllable — is regarded as the standard, as is
the case in French. In Italian, on the contrary, the
great majority of the words are stressed on the next-
to-last syllable; and therefore the feminine line —
the one accented on the penult — is taken as the
normal type.

> Però ch' amore no se po vedére
> E no si trata corporaleménte,
> Manti ne son de sì fole sapére
> Che credono ch'amor sïa nïénte.

Moreover, Italian (in this respect closer to English
than is Provençal) has not a few words stressed on
the third syllable from the end, a type exceedingly
rare in the idioms of France. Hence a dactyllic measure at the cæsura in Italian corresponds naturally
enough to a trochaic one in Provençal. Compare
"Nos jove ómne, quandius qu'e nos estám" and
"Rosa fresc' aulentíssima ch'appar in ver l'estáte."

In reckoning the syllables, both languages follow
the general principle that contiguous vowels, unless
they belong to very distinctly separate syllables in

the same word, count as one; but this principle is applied with less laxity in Italian, where nearly all the words end in vowels, than in Provençal, where consonantal endings are common. Provençal may have, and often has, such combinations as "ños jove omne," in which the final *e* and the initial *o* count separately, whereas in Italian such a phrase as "del giovinetto anno" is scarcely conceivable without a fusion of the *o* and the *a*.

On the other hand, Provençal is much stricter than Italian with regard to absolute identity of vowel sounds in the rime. The former does not tolerate a coupling of close *e* with open *è*, or close *ó* with open *ò: vér* may not rime with *fèr*, nor *amór* with *còr*. The latter allows them with perfect freedom: *féde chiède, stélla bèlla, amóre còre, sólo duòlo.* It even admits a matching of surd and sonant *s*, as *cosa osa*. The explanation of this strange license is to be found, possibly, in the variations of pronunciation in the sundry dialects and in the literary medium.

The line, in Provençal, might be of any length, from one syllable to fourteen syllables, although some types are of course very much commoner than others. This seems to have been the case also in the earliest Italian verse; but there presently arose a tendency to prefer eleven-syllable and seven-syllable lines to all others. Dante, in his *De Vulgari Eloquentia,* surveying the work of his predecessors, declares

the eleven-syllable verse to be the finest and by far
the most frequent; next comes the seven-syllable
line, which may be mingled with the eleven-syllable,
to the advantage of the latter. After that come
the five-syllable and the three-syllable. The nine-
syllable and all kinds of lines with an even number
of syllables have, according to him, never been much
used in Italy.

The lyric stanza, as Dante describes it in this
same work, regularly is divided into two sections,
one or the other of which is subdivided into two
parts by a repetition in the music and the rimes.
If the first section is divided, its parts are called *feet*,
and the undivided second section is called a *train* or
tail. If the second section is divided, its parts are
verses, and the united first section is a *brow*. Some
kinds of lyrics, such as the *sestina*, have no division.
This principle of tripartition of the stanza, by the
way, though conspicuous in Italian poetry from the
beginning, is by no means characteristic of the songs
of Provence.

This stanza from one of the so-called Sicilian
poets, Giacomino Pugliese, has a *brow* and two
verses:

Brow. Death, why dost thou afflict me with such pain,
  Stealing my love, and with her all my mirth?
The flower of earthly beauty hast thou slain;
  Now have I naught to live for, here on earth.
Verse. Discourteous Death, to treat my pleading so!
  Thou 'st parted lovers, frozen pleasure's glow,
    Till all is sad.

Verse. My former gayety is turned to woe,
For thou hast killed all comfort here below,
Which once I had.

In the following strophe from a passionate love-
poem by Dante, we have two *feet* and a *tail:*

Foot.   No shield can screen me from her shattering blow,
From her pursuing gaze I vainly flee.
As flower on stem, so she
Perches upon my mind with conquering smile.
Foot.   She seems as heedful of my bitter woe
As ship seems heedful of a waveless sea.
The weight that crushes me
Is far beyond the scope of any style.
[Translation from *The Ladies of Dante's Lyrics*, 65–66.]

It will be noted that the second *foot* has the same
rimes as the first. Then comes the *tail* or *train* (*coda*
or *sirima*), with a new set of endings, but linked to
the *feet* by one rime:

O pitiless and agonizing file,
Which silently dost wear my life away,
Art not ashamed to stay
And gnaw my heart to dust from peel to peel,
As I'm ashamed to tell whence comes thy zeal?
[*Così nel mio parlar*, 2d stanza:
translation from *The Ladies of Dante's Lyrics*, 94.]

This poem offers a good example of the mingling —
of course according to a regular pattern — of seven-
syllable with eleven-syllable lines:

Non trovo scudo ch'ella non mi spezzi,
Nè luogo che dal suo viso m'asconda.
Ma come fior di fronda,
Così della mia mente tien la cima.

Now, when Dante, as a boy and youth in the busy, prosperous, rapidly expanding city of Florence — which, having quickly grown rich, was starting on a career of refinement and eager cultivation of the arts — when Dante, in such an environment, first turned his attention seriously to poetry, it was natural that, following the new fashion of his day, he should plunge into vernacular song rather than into the Latin verse of the ancients and their imitators. Of course he early began to read Latin poetry (Virgil being the principal textbook in medieval schools), and before the end of his life — probably long before — he acquired the art of writing it. In 1320 or thereabouts a noteworthy classicist of Bologna sent him a letter in Latin verse, reproving him courteously for consigning his ideas to a vulgar dialect rather than to the recognized medium of scholarship, urging him to write a Latin epic, and holding out the prospect of a laurel crown from the university. Dante answered in an elaborate eclogue, fashioned in a general way on the model of Virgil. His correspondent returned to the attack in another eclogue, begging Dante to visit Bologna; and Dante excused himself in a third. Dante's eclogues, though less fluent and polished than those which Petrarch wrote, considerably later, show much skill in handling Latin prosody. There is an early tradition that he first began the *Divine Comedy* in Latin hexameters. At any rate, he may well have contem-

plated the use of that language, which he employed
in all his prose works except the *New Life* and the
Banquet, and considered in connection even with
these.

Why did he choose to be a vernacular rather than
a classical poet, after he had reached his prime and
had steeped himself in Latin poetry? Petrarch was
confronted with the same problem, and solved it by
trying to excel in both languages, setting greater
store, however, by his Latin than by his Italian
verses. Perhaps Dante never felt sufficiently at
home in the ancient tongue to give free rein to his
imagination in that medium; possibly, by the time
he had completed his literary studies, he felt himself
committed to Italian, or indissolubly attached to it,
as he tells us in the *Banquet.* He may, too, have
been influenced by a thought which Petrarch afterwards expressed in one of his letters: "The Latin,"
he says, "in both prose and poetry, is undoubtedly
the nobler language, but for that very reason it has
been so thoroughly developed by earlier writers that
neither we nor anyone else may expect to add much
to it. The vernacular, on the other hand, has but
recently been discovered, and, though it has been
ravaged by many, it still remains uncultivated, in
spite of a few earnest laborers, and still shows itself
capable of much improvement and enrichment."
Whatever the cause may have been, Dante, as far as
we absolutely know, composed no classic Latin verse

except the two eclogues; and these he wrote, doubtless, mainly to prove that he could do it if he tried.

There is one other style of Latin poetry, current in the later Middle Ages, that might conceivably have interested Dante: namely, a kind of song, religious or secular, built on the same plan as the vernacular lyrics. This type, apparently, he never attempted. Provençal verse, in which some Italian poets before him had been proficient, he tried only in the instance previously mentioned. French, the language in which his elderly friend and adviser, Brunetto Latini, wrote his most famous book, Dante, as far as we know, never wrote, although he surely read it. In maturity as in youth he remained faithful to Italian versification.

The question immediately suggests itself: was he as great an innovator in prosody as in language; did he contribute the "improvement or enrichment" of which Petrarch speaks; did he create or refashion or expand the technique of Italian poetry as by his choice and accumulation and use of words he provided his fellow countrymen with a literary vocabulary? It must be admitted that here his influence was not nearly so important. The structure of verse was well established before his time — far more developed than the language itself — and he took it, in the main, as he found it. Still, if we look closely at his work and that of his followers, we can detect his mark, though it be a faint one.

The structure of the lyric stanza he theoretically regularized, as we have seen, confining it to three general types, while admitting great variety in length and in the number and arrangement of the rimes. Here his influence, if any he had, was corrective rather than creative, and, after lyric poetry in general ceased to be sung (being no longer written to music), his restrictions in large measure lost their reason for existence. It is quite conceivable that the forms of lyric verse to-day might be what they are, had Dante never lived. One cannot say the same of the pattern he used in the *Divine Comedy*, the *terza rima;* for that he apparently invented himself, and bequeathed it to posterity. When Dante first planned the composition of a long narrative and didactic poem in the vulgar tongue, he had the choice of several models. Historical songs in French and Provençal were written in *laisses:* that is, in sections, of varying length, in which all the lines rime or assonate together; but this form would hardly have come under Dante's consideration. Romantic tales and didactic works, when in verse, were composed in rimed couplets, both in northern and in southern France; so wrote the Italian Sordello, so likewise (in Italian) Dante's adviser, Brunetto Latini. The author of the *Fiore*, an abridged Italian paraphrase of the Old French *Romance of the Rose*, wrote in stanzas, each of which is a sonnet; some think (be it said in passing) that this author

was none other than Dante himself. We know that
Dante did write — for although the poem is lost, he
tells us so, in the *New Life* — an enumeration of the
sixty fairest ladies in Florence, in a form called
serventese, a series of short stanzas made up of three
long lines and one little one, the short final line of
each stanza riming with the three long lines of the
next. Dante, for his great work, chose none of these,
but devised, it would seem, from the *serventese* a sequence of groups of three lines in which the first and
third of each group rime together, while the middle
one rimes with the first and third of the following
group.

> Mid-course along our life's allotted way,
>> Within a murky wood my mind grew clear:
>> Far from the path my feet had gone astray.
> Ah me! a dreadful thing to write — how drear,
>> How wild, how waste a look that woodland wore,
>> The thought of which to-day renews my fear!
> So bitter 't is, that death is scarcely more;
>> But if the happy ending I would tell,
>> I needs must speak of things I saw before.
>
> *[Inf.,* I, 1–9.]

A form really marvelous in its union of continuity
with pause, of unity with change.

The tendency to restrict individual lines to two
types, those of eleven and of seven syllables, was by
him carried so far that only one of his lyrics, *Poscia
ch' Amor del tutto m'ha lasciato* (rather a poor poem,
by the way), contains verses of any different length.

One other ode sometimes ascribed to him, but probably not his, *Morte poich' io non truovo a cui mi
doglio*, has in each stanza two lines of five syllables.
This restriction to two measures, which on the whole
was pretty generally approved until the nineteenth
century, lent coherence and dignity to the lyric
strophe, but curtailed its variety. In the *canzone*
Dante set nobility and majesty above sprightly
sparkle. The dominant eleven-syllable line affords,
in itself, a good deal of diversity, as Dante uses it;
for its internal accent may fall at will on the fourth
syllable or the sixth, there being no cæsura. This
practice had grown up before Dante, who established it for good and all. Hence we may find two
successive lines such as

<blockquote>
Nel mezzo del cammin di nostra vita
Mi ritrovai per una selva oscura,
</blockquote>

accented 6–10 and 4–10.

In the reckoning of syllables, Dante, though not
absolutely rigid, was more systematic than his
predecessors. It would be tiresome to go into tech-
nical details; but in a general way it may be said
that he usually confined hiatus — the separate
counting of two or more adjacent vowels — to two
cases: if the vowels were in different words, they
might be separated if the first was the word *a* or the
word *e* or the word *o*, or if the first vowel was accented, as in

<blockquote>
Poi si tornò | all' eterna fontana;
</blockquote>

if they were in the same word, they might count
separately if the word in question was felt to be a
Latinism, as *cosc̈ienza* in

> Se non che consc̈ienza m' assicura.

Sometimes two counts are given for other reasons, as
for a lingering utterance or for slow impressiveness.
Such liberty as Dante wisely retained — a greater
freedom than is enjoyed by modern poets — he put
to artistic use in giving the effect of a swift or a
solemn movement. In one particularly majestic
passage, near the close of the *Paradise*, the fre-
quency of hiatus produces a distinctly *ritardando*
result in the *tempo*.

The dissyllabic rime Dante kept as a norm, regarding, however, words like *hai, noi, via* — which
in the interior of the line are monosyllabic — as
dissyllables when they stand at the end:

> Che la verace via abbandonaï . . .
> Inde si mosse un lume verso noï . . .
> Non era lunga ancor la nostra vïa . . .

Occasionally Dante broke the monotony by a monosyllabic or a trisyllabic rime, but one cannot be sure
that he always had a purpose in so doing, because
often no reason is evident for placing the irregular
endings in one spot rather than in another.

> "Io son Virgilio, e per null' altro rio
> Lo ciel perdei, che per non aver fè."
> Così rispose allora il Duca mio.

Qual è colui che cosa innanzi sè
  Subita vede, ond' ei si maraviglia,
  Che crede e no, dicendo: "Ell' è, non è,"
Tal parve quegli . . .

[*Purg.*, VII, 7–13.]

Such lines as these in *fè, sè, è*, which make an abrupt
break in the smooth current, are called *versi tronchi*,
"cut-off verses." In Dante and the other old poets,
however, it is generally doubtful whether the rimes
in question were really monosyllabic; for *fè, sè, è* and
the like, at the end of a phrase, were commonly
sounded *fèe, sèe, èe*, etc. In this particular passage
monosyllabic end-words would come in appropriately enough, to suggest startled surprise. A contrary effect is produced by the *versi sdruccioli*,
"sliding verses," which close with a rime of three
syllables.

Su per lo scoglio prendemmo la via,
  Ch' era ronchioso, stretto e malagevole,
  Ed erto più assai che quel di pria.
Parlando andava per non parer fievole;
  Onde una voce uscìo dall' altro fosso,
  A parole formar disconvenevole.

[*Inf.*, XXIV, 61–66.]

"We resumed our way over the ridge, which was
craggy, narrow, and difficult, and steeper far than
the one before. I talked as I climbed, in order not
to seem feeble — whereupon there issued from the
next ditch a voice unsuited to shape words." The
voice in question is the voice of a snake; and the

"sliding lines" may result from a subconscious reaction to the idea of proximity to a ditch full of ser-
pents. But sometimes we have not even such a clue
as this.

The *versi sdruccioli* Dante avoided in his lyrics;
they were not recognized as a regular type until the
fifteenth century, when they were used by Boiardo
in an eclogue and later by Sannazaro in some of the
poems of his *Arcadia*. Of the *versi tronchi* I find
among Dante's short poems only one example — a
ballad, in which one line in each stanza, and in the
chorus, ends monosyllabically. Here is the chorus:

> Per una ghirlandetta
> Ch' io vidi, mi farà
> Sospirare ogni fiore.

The second and third end-words of this refrain rime
with lines in the stanzas that follow.

In the matter of riming close and open vowels,
Dante followed the established practice. Here was
a chance for reform, in the interest of perfect harmony of sound; but Dante attempted no change, nor
do we know that He ever thought of such a thing. In
English we are not much disturbed by such tradi-
tional rimes as *heaven* and *given*, *find* and *wind*, *bear*
and *hear*, *made* and *said*, *down* and *known*, *head* and
deed, *move* and *love*, *worth* and *forth* — all of which I
came across in two nineteenth-century poets in five
minutes' reading. These, however, are individual
words, — although some of them do fall into cate-

gories, — whereas the license which Dante adopted
and passed on affects two great classes, comprising
a considerable part of the language. The imperfection in Italian, on the other hand, is slighter than
that illustrated by some of the English cases just
cited: it is comparable to a mating of *head* and *sad*,
or of *note* and *caught*, with this difference, that the
Italian rimed vowels are alike to the eye. It is certain that the diversity of sounds existed in Dante's
speech, for it comes straight down from Latin to the
Tuscan of to-day; but it is not marked by the spell-
ing. One should remember that in pronouncing
Latin the Italians nowadays habitually give the
open sound to all the *e*'s and *o*'s; if this was the practice in Dante's time (and there is some reason to
believe it was), this usage may have suggested the
idea that the open sound, being Latin and therefore
nobler and more "grammatical," was preferable,
even in vernacular poetry. That is, Dante and his
contemporaries, while they ordinarily pronounced
côda and *frôda*, may, in reading or singing verse,
have said *còda* and *fròda*. With regard to surd and
sonant *s*, as in *naso* and *caso*, we cannot be absolutely sure what the current usage was in the
Florence of the thirteenth and fourteenth centuries.
There have certainly been some changes in the pronunciation of *z;* there may have been more for *s*.

Assuming, however, that these suppositions are
unfounded, that Dante really and consciously rimed

mȇssa and *confèssa,* *côda* and *fròda, naso* and *caso,*
we must conjecture that he cared less for precision
in his endings than for the widest possible choice of
rime-words, even in a language as rich in rimes as
Italian. This view is supported by his occasional
coupling of a single with a double consonant, as in
vòto and *galeòtto, scêmi* and *dièmmi, sospêsi* and
compiêssi, a defect but slightly mitigated by the un-
stable orthography of those early days, which sometimes wrote double consonants single. In some
cases, too, the consonant may actually have been
pronounced single in his speech. It seems likely
that Dante's artistic instinct tended toward freedom
in rime, while in the length of lines and in the structure of the stanza it tended in the opposite direction,
toward standardization. His practice, except for the
rare confusion of single and double consonants, has
persisted down to our time.

One more thing is to be noted with regard to
Dante's rimes: we find in the *Divine Comedy* an unmistakable liking for odd and unexpected rime-
words. Very often, of course, the choice is determined by the exigencies of the case: frequently no
familiar rime-word could be found. But there are
instances enough in which the strange word could
easily have been avoided. *Per li,* "over the," riming
with *merli* and *piacerli; almen tre,* "at least three,"
riming with *entre* and *ventre; o me,* "ah me," riming
with *come* and *chiome* — these illustrate one kind of

eccentricity. The sequence *Etïòpe*, *inòpe*, *pròpe*, all un-Italian words, is an example of another. In an old literature it is natural to shun overworked and threadbare rimes, such as *youth* and *truth*, *beauty* and *duty*, *ocean* and *motion;* but in a poet who stands, as Dante does, close to the beginning of the poetry of his nation, the desire for new and startling rimes is significant.

Another peculiarity of the verse of the *Divine Comedy* is its abundant use of alliteration.

*N*el *m*ezzo del cam*m*in di *n*ostra vita . . .	n – n, m – m
E *qu*anto a *d*ir *qu*al era è cosa *d*ura . . .	qu – qu, d – d
Che *n*el *p*ensier rin*n*ova la *p*aura.	n – n, p – p
Tanto è a*m*ara che *p*oco è più *m*orte.	m – m, p – p
Ma per *tr*attar del ben ch' i' *v*i *tr*ovai . . .	tr – tr, v – v

These are five of the first eight lines of the *Inferno;* and in these eight lines I have confined myself to the perfectly obvious examples. Each of the five, it will be observed, has a double alliteration. In a very large proportion of Dante's lines alliteration occurs, single or double. According to Professor Garlanda of Rome, who wrote a book on Dante's versification, these harmonies of consonants are a regular factor in our poet's scheme, as much as the rimes. One need not go quite so far as that. Many of the consonant identities are doubtless accidental (as they are in the words I have just written, *identities* and *doubtless* and *accidental*); it would indeed be next to impossible to write either poetry or prose that should be without them. But their great number and their very frequent occurrence at the beginning of the most important words in the line show that their effect must have been more or less calculated by the author. With the alliterations we may class repetitions, or echoes, such as *selva selvaggia*, "wild wilderness"; *io fui per ritornar più volte volto*, "full many a *t*ime I *t*urned me to go back," where a simple alliteration seems to be the best one can do in English; or again, *perchè fur negletti Li nostri vóti e vòti in alcun canto*, "because neglected were our *v*ows and *v*oid in some respect."

One more observation, and we are done. I have said that Italian poetry, like that of the other Romance languages, is not constructed, as is English and German verse, on the principle of regular beats, or a systematic alternation of strong and weak. In the *Divine Comedy*, however, we find a greater approximation to such rhythm than in the poets before or after Dante. Professor Garlanda, indeed, has tried to work out for the *Commedia* a regular accentual scheme. Such a line as *Amór condússe nói ad úna mórte* is as rigidly metrical as "Téll me nót in móurnful númbers"; and *Nel mézzo del cammín di nóstra vita* is parallel to "Lífe is but an émpty dréam," each of these two lines really skipping one beat.

To form a just estimate of these æsthetic factors, one would have to study a great number of Dante's lines. Yet merely by reading observantly the exquisite little passage below one gains an inkling of the master's art — of his varying yet constant metrical flow, of the sweetness of his rimes, of his subtle and pervasive alliterations, of his rhythmical but not rigorously schematic accentuation.

> O animal grazioso e benigno,
>   Che visitando vai per l' aer perso
>   Noi che tignemmo il mondo di sanguigno,
> Se fosse amico il re dell' universo,
>   Noi pregheremmo lui della tua pace,
>   Poichè hai pietà del nostro mal perverso.
> Di quel che udire e che parlar ti piace
>   Noi udiremo e parleremo a vui,
>   Mentrechè il vento, come fa, ci tace.
>
> [*Inf.*, v, 88–96.]

Chapter IX

LOST POEMS OF DANTE

" AFTER speaking these words, Love vanished, because of the great share of himself that he seemed to have given me" (*Vita Nuova*, chap. IX). That is, the God of Love (whom I had met on the road), after conversing with me and bidding me shift my heart from one lady to another, disappeared, because I absorbed so much of Love that there remained not enough to be seen. A strange and disconcerting conceit to encounter in plain prose! And never, I believe, should we have seen it in prose, had not Dante previously devised it in verse. At the close of the sonnet where it first appeared, it falls aptly into place, novel though it be:

Riding along one day, with burdened breast,
　Upon a road that cost me many a frown,
　I met with Love, who journeyed toward the town,
In habit like a pilgrim lightly drest.
His look was that of some one sore distrest;
　He seemed a monarch who has lost his crown,
　As sighing mournfully he came adown,
With face, to shun remark, netherward prest.
Beholding me, he called to me by name.
　"I come," he said, "afar from over there,
　　Where dwelt thy heart, as once I bade it do.
　Now here I bring it, new delight to woo."
Then I absorbed of him so great a share,
He disappeared.　God knows what he became!
　　　　　　　　[*The Ladies of Dante's Lyrics*, 36.]

Only in the prose paraphrase does the figure appear so startling. Inasmuch as the prose precedes the verse, as it regularly does in the *Vita Nuova*, nothing prepares us for a turn so whimsical; at first, we scarcely understand. And this is not the only time. Again and again, in Dante's "little book," we meet in the introductory paragraphs a phrase or a fancy that would doubtless never have occurred even to him, if he had thought out his matter originally in prosaic form. The burning heart of the third chapter really needs for its clarification the ensuing sonnet. Without the verse that follows, the discussion of the contradictions of love in Chapter XIII might seem a bit inane. The account of the poet's vision, in Chapter XLI, is poor and pale until the supremely beautiful closing sonnet gives it color.

On the other hand, it sometimes happens that the prose argument throws a needed light on the poem. Were it not for the long narrative that introduces the second *canzone*, we should hardly know what to make of this song of a feverish dream. The pretty story of the poet drawing a picture of angels, on the anniversary of his lady's death, absorbed in his task, while "men worthy of receiving honor" watch him unnoticed, informs us of the occasion of the sonnet in Chapter XXXIV, which the verses themselves in no wise suggest. Nor does the next-to-last sonnet in the book contain in itself all the elements of the scene that evoked it — the band of pilgrims marching

eager and absent-minded through the city of bereavement, on their way to Rome, to behold the
Veronica. Had we not the prose, we should not
know that her father's death was the cause of
Beatrice's mourning, so touchingly told in the sonnet-dialogue of Chapter XXII.

Not infrequently, indeed, the author, intent on a
mystic interpretation of his own early life and early
verse, insinuates into his prefatory remarks an idea
or a circumstance which is not to be found in the
accompanying poem, and presumably was not in the
poet's consciousness when he wrote it. The Dante
who collected some of his scattered lyrics and furnished them with a running explanation, at the age
of twenty-eight or so, was a Dante much changed
from his younger self, already a philosopher in
mood, a seeker for hidden meanings and correspond-
ences. The first sonnet, for instance, contains no
hint of impending death, which, in the light of the
subsequent event, its concluding words seemed to
forebode. In the little poem on Dante's encounter
with the God of Love there is no thought of Beatrice, with whom the prose nevertheless connects it.
Only by a feint of baffling dexterity is she linked,
in the commentary, with the elegy on the fair lady
who died young (Chapter VIII), or with the grief
expressed in the short *canzone* on the death of another lady, a friend of Beatrice's brother (Chapter
XXXIII). Of the occult fitness of the names Prima-

vera and Giovanna the young songster apparently
had no inkling when he composed his pretty sonnet
on Monna Vanna and Monna Bice (Chapter xxiv).
The number nine, on which such portentous emphasis is laid in the prose, is absent from the poems
which the author-editor selected for his book.

In one passage (Chapter vi) Dante does mention a composition of his, a *serventese* enumerating
the sixty prettiest ladies of Florence, wherein the
name of Beatrice was ninth. This poem is lost.
Perhaps the author did his best to suppress it, deem-
ing it out of harmony with his devotional temper
and his allegiance to Beatrice, which he subse-
quently chose to regard as constant during his boyish years, from eight to twenty-five. A paragraph
of terse prose tells us the subject of this piece of
verse — written in honor of the lady who stared at
the young poet in church — and divulges the reason
why mention is made of it, namely, that the number
nine is there associated with "the most gentle one."
Probably enough, as I have suggested elsewhere, the
whole idea of a mysterious connection between
Beatrice and nine arose from the chance which gave
her the ninth place in this roll, and from the writer's
desire to justify his apparent preference of other
charmers by finding in the order of his list a secret
predestined significance.

One thing is clear in the puzzling *Vita Nuova* —
seemingly so simple, really so complex: the work is

essentially an apology for the author's youthful conduct and a justification of his youthful poetry. Some
of Dante's best lyrics, current in Florence, were
manifestly designed for Beatrice; others just as manifestly were not. To bring these others into some relation with his chosen lady in such a way as to show
her always supreme — this was his problem. Some
of these other poems were too good to set aside;
these had to be included and interpreted. Such are
the elegies above mentioned and the sonnets to the
gentle lady at the window. Some, we may suppose,
could not be satisfactorily explained, or were not
worth the trouble, although, being well known, they
called for some recognition. Such is our *serventese;*
such the "little things in rime" which the poet tells
us he composed in celebration of that lady — the
lady of the church — to whom, through a period of
several years, he paid court in order to hide his love
for Beatrice. Whether any of these "little things"
are among the miscellaneous lyrics that have come
down to us, nobody can tell. A few of the preserved
sonnets and ballads can be as well attached to her as
to anyone else. For the other lady, the second whom
he used as a screen, the one whose reputation suf-
fered from his assiduous attentions, he must have
had recourse to rime. Have we any poetic record of
that wooing?

Similar doubts arise concerning the gentle lady at
the window. Surely the author wrote more verse

for her than the four sonnets included in the *Vita
Nuova*. Is most of it gone, or have we a considerable
part of it among the unattached *Rime*? Are we to
restore to her the poems devoted to Lady Philosophy, especially the first and second *canzoni* of the
Convivio; or were these really composed after the
pitying young woman had ceased to be more than
a symbol?

Did Dante ever reply to Guido Cavalcanti's sonnets, addressed to him, *I' vegno il giorno, Se vedi
Amore, Dante un sospiro*? Or to Cino's sonnet,
Dante i' ho preso l'abito di doglia? Or to these three
by Cecco Angiolieri: *Dante Allaghier, Cecco, 'l tu'
servo e amico; Lassar vo' lo trovare di Becchina; Dante
Allaghier, s'i' son bon begolardo*? To the first of
these, indeed, Dante made sufficient answer in the
prose of Chapter XLI of the *Vita Nuova*. Where is
Dante's poem to which Guido Orlandi responded in
his sonnet, *Poi che traesti infino al ferro l'arco*?

Now, as we read the *Vita Nuova* with such queries
and such facts in mind, we have the feeling that certain incidents of the prose text must have been first
told in verse, that certain paragraphs were meant to
interpret sundry lyrics which are not there. In some
cases this feeling is vague, in others it amounts almost to certainty. For his omission of many poems
Dante had not only the reasons conjectured above,
but also the necessities of his symmetrical plan,
which called for a prearranged grouping of matter

and of form. That he did sometimes discard, he avers explicitly; but he discloses nothing definite about the extent of his exclusions. It will be an interesting pastime to guess the places which reflect absent verse, and to speculate on its nature; for there is always pleasure in study and surmise, when the subject is Dante.

One of the problematic passages greets us as soon as we open the book — the ambiguous statement regarding the lady's name: "she was called Beatrice (or Blesser) by many *i quali non sapeano che si chiamare*," that is, apparently, either "who knew not what to call her" or "who knew not what they were calling." The author seems to have desired to leave in the reader's mind a doubt whether Beatrice was a descriptive appellation or a real name, miraculously fit. While the theme lends itself easily to versified treatment in the punning or riddle style so often affected by medieval versifiers, there is no clear indication of a poem here.

To the age at which the future poet first met the little Bice, there is reference in one of his sonnets to Cino da Pistoia, *Io sono stato con Amore insieme;* and of the tremendous effect of her coming, upon Dante's "spirits" (as told in Chapter II), we find a reflection in one of the *canzoni, E' m'incresce di me sì malamente,* in the fifth and sixth stanzas:

> The day this lady came into the world, —
> As still is clearly shown
> In memory's book, which fadeth fast away, —

Into my tiny, helpless form was hurled
 A passion all unknown,
 Which kept me filled with quivering dismay.
 A check was put on all my powers that day
So suddenly that straight to earth I fell,
 Hearing a voice, which fearful smote my breast
If truth the book do tell,
 My greatest spirit quaked, with shortened breath,
 So hard, 't was plain that death
 Had come to earth to be that spirit's guest.
 Now Love, who did it all, is sore distrest.

Then, later, when I saw her beauteous face,
 The source of all my harm,
 (Fair listening ladies, who avoid me not!)
That faculty which hath the highest place,
 Considering her charm,
 Clearly perceived its miserable lot
And recognized the longing that was got
By one sweet lingering look her eyes did cast;
 And thus addrest the other faculties:
"Who once was here, is past!
 Henceforth that lovely figure shall I see
 Which now doth frighten me;
 And over all of us, when it shall please
 Her queenly eyes, the sceptre she shall seize."
    [*The Ladies of Dante's Lyrics*, 109, 110.]

Is the curiously pedantic prose of the middle part of
the second chapter based on a previous poetic treatment, fuller than the above? Who shall say?

Next comes the first greeting, so prettily conceived, and in such detail, that we may be sure the
scene was vividly pictured in the lover's mind, even
if he did not reduce it to verse. The poem which
closes the chapter (Chapter III) portrays not the

salutation, but a mysterious ensuing dream. The encounter itself falls quite as readily into rime as into prose:

Since first we met, the years had numbered nine
　　When, walking slow, two gentle dames between,
　　The Gentlest One, at Love's behest, I ween,
Came onward till her steps encountered mine.
Tho' timorously mine eyes I did incline,
　　Her wondrous presence none the less was seen;
　　I saw her face, her garments' snowy sheen;
I saw her eyes like stars of heaven shine.
Then smilingly she bent her radiant gaze
　　Upon her slave, who stood disconsolate.
With kindness that deserves eternal praise
　　　　She spake to me in sweet and modest tone.
　　Eager my happiness to meditate
　　　　And drunk with joy, I took my way alone.

If the first part of Chapter III is so suggestive of poesy that the presumptuous translator can hardly keep to prose, the whole of Chapter IV almost inevitably turns him willy-nilly into a rimester. In fact, this little chapter is scarcely explicable save as the paraphrase of a poem — let us say, this time, a ballad:

What time my envious friends would fain have heard
　　The name of her who maketh me to pine,
　　In answer to their mischievous design,
I smiled at them, and never spake a word.

Pining away in amorous distress
　　Weak with the feebleness which love attends,
　　　　So sadly was my natural spirit tried,
　　The sight of me was grievous to my friends.

And when they asked me, full of eagerness,
　　What sickness had my flesh so mortified,
　　I told them, "Love"; for that I could not hide.
Of all that rule below or rule above,
　　No master marks his slaves so plain as Love.
A feigned reply had therefore been absurd.

But when my envious friends would fain have heard
　　The name of her who maketh me to pine,
　　In answer to their mischievous design,
I smiled at them, and never spake a word.

Doubt changes to quasi-conviction when we reach
the episode of the church (Chapter v). Is it over-
venturesome to imagine how this incident might
have been set forth in rime? After all, to translate
Dante's prose into English verse is no more audacious than to take the same liberty with his poetry.

Hide as I would from men my pallid face,
　　Their questioning eyes did still examine me
　　And cast anon a secret look at thee,
As with the crowd I issued from a place
Where words were spoken of the Queen of Grace.
　　As forth they fared, they turned their heads to see,
　　And, whispering, stared with curious scrutiny;
For on my features Love had left his trace.
"How doth yon lady make this man to pine!"
　　Was muttered more than once in murmur soft;
　　Because mine eyes, which erst had lookt aloft,
Were led by Love, within that holy shrine,
　　To seek thine eyes, intently and full oft,
Until thy gaze responsive answered mine.

As to the *serventese* (Chapter vi), with its record
of sixty beautiful Florentines, probably with the first

lady of concealment at the head, and certainly with
Beatrice in the ninth place, what can it have been?
Dante calls it an "epistle." Was it merely a list with
brief characterizations, or was it an allegorical narrative, like the *Chariot* of Raimbaut de Vaqueiras?
This Provençal songster had been entertained, a
century before Dante, by the Malaspina family, and
did homage to a Lady Beatrice of Monferrat. His
poem is a ladies' battle. The fair ones of the city,
jealous of the fairest, declare war against her and
gather in a host, affording the chronicler a chance
for enumeration; but are routed, foot and horse, by
Beatrice. Or did Alighieri prefer the fancy of Bertran de Born, who, scorned by his adored, would
seek comfort in a synthetic sweetheart, composed of
the various charms of the ladies he knew? It is more
likely that our poet's imagining took the shape of a
visionary pageant, a procession of loveliness led by
Love himself. Such a poem might have begun in
this vein:

> To all that heed our Master's bidding well
> A vision of fair ladies now I tell,
> Of sixty queens who all in Florence dwell,
>   A goodly sight.
> The vision came to me on yesternight.
> First Love appeared, a figure clad in white;
> And Mistress Joan was marching on his right,
>   With golden hair.
> And on his left was Lisbeth, wondrous fair;
> And Adelaide, with laughing eyes, was there;
> Matilda, too, who sings beyond compare,
>   That winsome maid.

A tragic happening, left unversified in the *New Life*, is the refusal of her salutation by the "most gentle one," a loss whose bitterness is brought home to us by a description of the wondrous effect of the lady's greeting.

> When I my Gentle One was near to meet,
>   My senses, all but sight, appeared to die,
>   And Love, instead of sight, possest mine eye,
> The better to receive her greeting sweet.
> All anger spent, with modesty replete,
>   My heart was lit by radiance from on high
>   And spake its gladness in a gentle sigh,
> When she her servitor vouchsafed to greet.
> Now all my gladsome pride is turned to shame.
>   No more do people say: "What fortunes bless
>   This man transformed, who walks beatified?"
> A foe to scandal, which befouls my name,
>   Her greeting hath my Gentle One denied,
>   Wherein resided all my happiness.

Following the story of the mockery of Beatrice and her lover's discomfiture at a wedding banquet, there is a sonnet, which contains, however, none of the detail elaborated in the introduction. This prose, indeed, tells us all we know of the circumstances under which Mistress Bice joined her companions in smiling at the poor figure cut by her bewildered admirer. Nevertheless, I do not believe there ever was a fuller treatment of the theme in verse. The minute prefatory narrative is needed to explain how it could happen that one so gentle as Beatrice should indulge in the *gabbo* which the sonnet rebukes, and how the serious Dante could have provoked laughter. Even with the prose, the episode is by no means clear. One is tempted to add things which the author did not care to state: for instance, that Beatrice and her young friends, having conceived the opinion that Dante was a flirt, took his emotion for mere amatory posturing; furthermore, that there was something incongruous in his leaning against the pictured wall of the apartment, a feature which he specifies in the prose and to which he vaguely refers in the verse of Chapter xv, where he declares that his swooning heart "leans wherever it can."

The *New Life* falls into three equal parts, the first of which closes with the author's conversion to the "new style" of love and poetry, which had its rise in imitation of Guido Guinizelli of Bologna, "the master of all those who have ever written sweet rimes of love." Now, this conversion is set forth tersely, baldly, and none too clearly, in a little chapter (Chapter xvii) which caps as an anticlimax the ascending series of three desperate sonnets that immediately precede. In similar fashion, the news of the death of Beatrice, which ends the second part of the book, is briefly and prosaically conveyed in Chapter xxviii, just after a *crescendo* arrangement of three little songs of supernaturally peaceful happiness.

Following Chapter xvii, the announcement of conversion, we have a detailed account of an inci-

dent which precipitated the change, namely, a
conversation with certain ladies who, aware of his
discomfitures, question the poet and criticize the in-
consistency of his theory with his practice. Though
fancifully told, the episode has all the air of a real
occurrence, and curiosity asks whether Dante ever
attempted to narrate it in verse. Some features of
the story are strongly suggestive of poetry: the
description of one of the ladies — the one who called
to Dante — as "possessed of right dainty speech"
— *donna di molto leggiadro parlare*; the picture of
the group, some laughing, some chatting together,
some looking at the young man expectantly; especially the figure of words and sighs issuing together
from their lips, "as sometimes we see water falling
mixed with pretty snow." On the other hand, we
have the pendant to this prose in the great *canzone*,
"Ladies who have intelligence of love." One may
perhaps assume that the prose story is elaborated
simply to explain the dedication of the poem to
gentle ladies. My guess, however, is that in the de-
vising of the *canzone* — a process that was long and
hard, as the author avows — his idea passed through
several phases, from a portrayal of the whole event
to an exemplification of its consequence. In this
case the dedication would be all that remains of the
original plan, while the poetic touches in the prose
would be remnants of this unrealized first conception.

After the brief announcement of the passing of Beatrice, in Chapter xxviii, we have a solemn discussion of the meaning of the number nine, which has constantly attached itself to her. In this I can see no sign of a poetic original, although the theme is one which Dante, in later life, might conceivably have treated in a rimed disquisition. As much may be said of Chapter xxv, which deals with personification as a rhetorical license.

First readers of the *Vita Nuova*, I think, are always taken aback when they discover that unadorned, laconic prose is chosen as a vehicle for the incident which would seem to form the natural climax of the whole book. The author, indeed, foresaw their surprise, and excused himself for the absence of the expected poem. Three reasons he alleges, the first and third of them far-fetched, the middle one frank and convincing enough — to wit, that "my tongue was not yet competent to treat fittingly thereof." That he tried the task again and again, there can be little doubt; and as far as one may surmise, his attempts took the form of a pilgrimage of his soul to Paradise to behold the glory of his lady — a dream that found perfect fulfilment only in the *Divine Comedy*. The *canzone* of Chapter xxxi, therefore, "My eyes which mourn for pity of my heart," does not represent the theme he conceived; for it treats of the bereavement of the earth, touching but incidentally on the heavenly assumption of Beatrice. As to the Latin composition (Chapter xxx) addressed to the "princes of the earth," we have no evidence that it was in verse. Dante's nearest approach to the expression of his idea, in his earlier years, is to be sought, not in a *canzone*, but in that beautiful sonnet with which he chose to conclude his *New Life: Oltre la spera che più larga gira:*

> Beyond the sphere which hath the loftiest gyre
>   Passes the sigh that issues from my breast;
>   A new intelligence which Love, distrest,
> Confers upon it, drives it ever higher.
> When it has reacht the goal of its desire,
>   It sees a lady, honored by the blest,
>   And shining so that, blindingly imprest,
> The pilgrim spirit lingers to admire.
> 'T is all so strange that when it tells me this
>   I cannot comprehend, it puzzles so
>   The mournful heart which ever bids it tell.
>   It speaketh of that gentle one, I know,
> Because it often nameth Beatrice;
>   And that, dear ladies mine, I hear full well.

Chapter X

SIX CENTURIES

1321–1921

HAS knowledge, waxing with increase of days,
   Informed the mind for better or for worse?
     Can mastery of matter reimburse
The soul for loss of faithful prayer and praise,
Revealing to our disillusioned gaze
     The vanity of blessing and of curse,
     And earth, once centre of the universe,
A casual atom in a boundless maze?
Or have we lost the more and gained the less
     Since, worshipers of science, we began
       To found our happiness on things we know?
Do beauty, honor, dignity progress?
       The grandest voice that ever spake from man
       Was still in death six hundred years ago.